CRAVING THE FUTURE

TRANSFORMING OUR DEEPEST DESIRES INTO NEW REALITIES

MICHAEL PERMAN

ISBN: 978-0-578-22205-9

Second Edition

For Jordana, Jacob, and Emily.

To all the soulful creatives "out there" wishing to shape the future.

Foreword

Michael Perman shares a unique body of wisdom derived from his extensive career as an innovation futurist and facilitator of creativity for large-scale organizations. This uniquely designed book will escort you on a delightful journey to create your personal and professional future through honest revelations, inspiring profiles of innovation luminaries, and extensive research about the relationship between human desire and creativity.

Michael believes that innovation is the ability to perceive alternative realities and the courage to move toward those visions. His research reveals that understanding what people crave in their lives—especially deep desires for sensations, experiences, purpose, and meaning—opens up our minds to perceive ideas that are often clouded by pre-conceived notions about what is possible.

Within these pages, I found that Michael's observations about the link between **CRAVING** and discovering new realities are fresh and intriguing. His ideas stimulate new thinking, and the last two chapters of the book provide pragmatic methods for driving your own future and moving ideas "from fuzzy to fruition," as he phrases it. **As I reflect on the chapters in my own life and the chapters that are ahead, having a toolkit for creating the future would be profoundly valuable.**

The innovative graphic approach to this book reflects Michael's extensive experience collaborating with designers to inform thinking and inspire creativity with insights and foresights. You will even find pages that provide a co-creative respite, with images and open spaces inviting your contributions. The book is designed to easily scan on your own and to use as a catalyst for team-building.

Whether you are in the midst of re-inventing your own personal future or wishing to lead and improve the future of the organization where you work, *CRAVING THE FUTURE* provides a generous helping of personal and professional wisdom for you to shape what is to come.

Chip Conley
Hospitality entrepreneur
Strategic advisor to Airbnb
Bestselling author

PREFACE

When I decided to write this book, experienced publishers advised me to share "a hero's journey." I loved that idea because I am a strong advocate of revealing narratives that connect Jungian archetypes in our personal lives with brands (for example, Nike is the Hero, Apple is the Creator, Disney is the Magician, Harley Davidson is the Outlaw, Levi's is the Explorer).

However, given the diversity of archetypes that exist in our culture, and my personal reality, I have come to the conclusion that I am not a hero and I do not have a hero's journey. I am actually not competitive, either. I have little personal need to win, prevail, or dominate.

My Jungian archetype is Explorer, which may explain my affection for the Levi's brand, where I worked as an executive for several years. My Explorer archetype also makes sense in concert with other organizational typographies, e.g., astrologically a Gemini, an INFP on the Meyers Briggs scale, a "five" in the Enneagram (the "Investigator," who "becomes preoccupied with thoughts and imaginary constructs").

Explorers seek authenticity, truth, and meaning. If there is any heroic act in my professional life, then it has been to lead a continuous journey to uncover insights, find answers, and mine new ideas, like a miner searching for gold in the original days of Levi's. To carve a new path in the road ahead, to see beyond the blue horizon. That is the work of an innovator; a constant search for the undiscovered and continuous odyssey for authentic revelations.

So, while I have navigated my share of personal adversity, I don't think of myself as a hero. I have helped dozens of organizations and people see the future differently, but those were not heroic acts—just acts of service to inspire creativity in other people, which I think of as my purpose in life.

This book is my gift to you, a multi-functional tool for your own journey into new realities (a journey where you will likely encounter adversity, doubt, and incredulous looks expressed through contorted eyebrows). As such, this book is an unfinished work, a prototype that is now open for your co-creation and exploration. I hope CRAVING THE FUTURE stimulates fresh thinking in your world.

Please share your thinking with me, and we can move ahead together in search of bold ideas that keep us traveling on our roads to authenticity.

INTRODUCTION

INNOVATION IS THE ABILITY TO PERCEIVE ALTERNATIVE **REALITIES** AND THE **COURAGE** TO MOVE TOWARD THOSE **VISIONS**.

Oy! I know what you're thinking. Another book about creativity and innovation?

If this is your first book on the subject, then congratulations! You picked the right book. If you are a master level innovator seeking fresh perspectives, then congratulations! You picked the right book.

At first, the alternative realities definition may seem a bit "out there" and psychedelic—at very least unconventional. Since I have lived in Marin County, California, and Portland, Oregon, you might easily think of my theory of alternative realities in its "out there" dimension. And frankly, it would be a fair assessment, since many people think I'm an "out there" thinker.

However, if you re-frame your interpretation as the ability to see alternatives to a current reality, then the definition may seem more practical.

The birth of Uber was an alternative to the reality of a cumbersome, uncomfortable method of obtaining and riding in a taxi cab. The genesis of Airbnb was an alternative to the reality of booking impersonal and cookie-cutter hotel rooms. Apple Pay or Venmo were alternatives to the reality of cash. You can even look back at the invention of the printing press and appreciate that it marked the beginning of broad communication, an alternative to the reality of written words being scribed one sheet at a time.

Think about the realities in your life, business, or organization, and how you are moving into the future. Which elements of your life are forever petrified and which elements are more pliable? If you already have a business or personal operating model that's working for you, then what risks and opportunities can you perceive that would change the model? How might you change the way you currently perceive and act upon your situation, so that your reality stops changing without your control?

Innovation emerges from you proactively witnessing the future that is unfolding around you and taking ownership of how that future becomes shaped. You could be passive or you could be active, but you certainly need to be attentive. Alan Kay, formerly a member of famed research organization Xerox PARC (Palo Alto Research Center), said it well, "The best way to predict the future is to invent it."

Thus, if you accept the premise of innovation being the ability to perceive alternative realities—and I hope you do—then how do you make that happen? How might you be enabled to perceive alternatives to current realities?

First, you need deep insights into human behavior and what is meaningful to people. You need a method to reveal insights well beyond the superficial expressions or diagnostic assessments of existing ideas that qualitative research often expresses.

In my experience, the ability to perceive alternative realities is derived from deeply understanding what people **CRAVE** in their lives—what they crave for a brighter future. In this context, craving is not merely defined by typical creature comforts, such as food, nor is it limited to nefarious addictions.

My interviews with more than 30 innovation luminaries, along with two quantitative surveys on the subject of craving, reveal that people crave much more than creature comforts in their lives. The spectrum of craving, which everyone I interviewed acknowledged, includes emotions, sensations, and a quest for meaningful purpose.

I personally crave smoked salmon and pastrami as creature comforts. They both remind me of my youth in Milwaukee, where my father was passionate about fish and the pastrami at our neighborhood deli delighted me.

But my deeper craving is to understand how our minds work, so that I am better prepared to see new possibilities. I believe that perceiving alternatives to current realities helps solve the challenges we face in life. Everyday challenges with families, friends, work, balance, and creativity.

I grew up in a family ethos of imaginative and abstract thinking. My father subscribed to the *Journal of Metaphysics* and the *Journal of Existentialism*. He was an expansive thinker who would often tell me "a solution exists for every problem in the world, but discovering that for your self is an elusive journey." So, it's no surprise that I like to think "out there." Our family also subscribed to the *New Yorker* magazine, and as a young child I collected dozens of their imaginative covers, taping them floor-to-ceiling, wall-to-wall in my bedroom, not necessarily reading them but just letting the abstract input expand my mental panorama.

The research my company conducted has revealed a wide spectrum of craving ideologies which you can read in Chapter 2 of this book. For example, Ivy Ross, head of design at Google, craves coherence and a sense awe. Katie Spotz, one of the world's most prolific endurance athletes, craves purpose and impact. Dr. Sue Morter, a human potential leader, thinks that many people crave wholeness. She believes "they're craving the entire complexity, the entire symphony. They're craving the experience of what full potential is. When it comes to creativity, they are craving remembering the truth of who we are."

Revealing what people crave comes from methodical inquiry and application, which we share in Chapter 5.

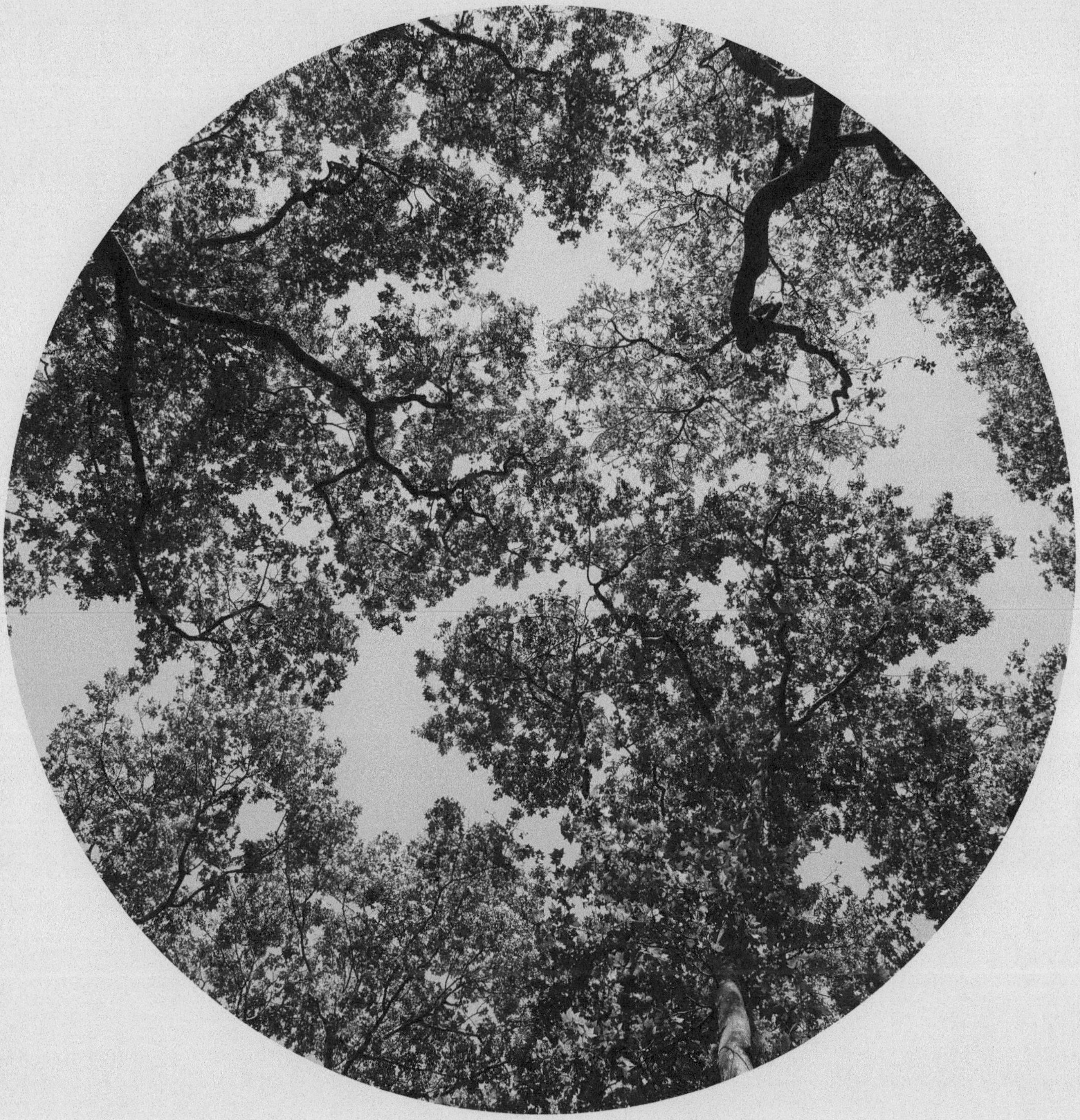

Now, what business book would be complete without an acronym? The **CRAVING** acronym is a method of inquiry to reveal what people are genuinely craving. We will put some meat on these bones in Chapter 3.

CURIOSITY: What elements do people wish to explore in new dimensions?

REFLECTION: Which memories people think and reflect on as the best moments in their lives?

AMBIGUITY: What do people seek even when the path and answers are unclear?

VORACITY: What experiences or feelings do people seek in unlimited amounts?

INNOVATION: What inspires people to experiment with new versions of what they love?

NOW: What might people wish for right now that would be extremely satisfying?

GENEROSITY: What motivates people to be generous and share their craving with others?

In short, your inquiry into craving is about what illuminates the human spirit. Understanding the fundamental elements of cravings among the people who are important in your life can lead to an abundant stream of happiness and delight. The experiences and feelings that people crave don't become tedious or tiring over time; they become richer and more interesting.

Once you understand what you or your community craves on a deeper level, then it is time to flex your muscles and generate future opportunities. Flexing your heart muscle of **empathy** to feel what people think leads to the level of creativity that is needed to be inventive or see new solutions for improvement, new realities.

Flexing your mind muscle of **curiosity** tunes your peripheral vision to explore an ambiguous landscape, to recognize patterns amidst seemingly disconnected ideas, and enables you to see what is coming beyond the blue horizon, around the corner where the nascent ideas are living under the radar.

Flexing empathy and curiosity sounds simple, right? Conceptually, yes, it is a simple proposition. However, there is another component. Innovation also requires the courage to move toward those visions and new realities you perceive.

Courage is derived from the intersection of empathy and curiosity—where your soulful core is tucked away, ready for nourishment

With innovation, courage is required to navigate the obstacles and overcome the objections *(we tried that, it's too early, far-fetched, not feasible, not on-strategy)*. Generating the ideas for innovation is relatively easy and methodical once you have expert-level facilitators. Our chapters at the end of this book provide step-by-step methods for generating ideas and concepts, and evolving them to brightness.

Generating ideas is the easy part of innovation and is often mistaken for the primary and iconic element. It's certainly a lot of fun and it is an important first step. And ideation can be delightful, meaningful, or both. But ideation is not the panacea of innovation. Along with foresights and insights, ideation is the genesis.

Courage is a core element of innovation because you need a lot of courage to manifest the visions and potential that creativity and foresight reveal. You will need to navigate complexity, deflect attacks on your perspective, circumvent premature operational thinking, and mollify the natural discomfort with ambiguity.

Transcending courage leads you to innovation with purpose. My purpose in life is to inspire creativity in other people. My mission in writing this book is to inspire your thinking and creativity with a combination of fresh perspective, insights from deep experience with innovation, evocative images, and practical advice that creates the right balance of magic, method, and memory. I admit, my views are often abstract and possibly ambiguous. Those qualities are inherent in innovation. That's why this book is a great "airplane read" or great for an excursion, where your mind can explore.

In this book I focus on the term "memory" as a tool for embedding the content. So, **your presence and mindful attention to the content and learning will help embed the methods and meaning in your mind for application in your real world**. Or, the perceived new reality.

Thus, we've made this book eminently consumable, quite digestible, and humbly imaginative. You should be able to cruise through this book on a train ride from Portland to Seattle, a plane ride from New York to Chicago, or three round trip rides on the San Francisco ferry from Marin into the city.

The following pages reveal contemporary perspectives on the concept of CRAVING and share ideas on how you might consider these perspectives in creating THE FUTURE. For even more insights about craving, connect to the CRAVING THE FUTURE podcast where you will hear about diverse themes from musicians, world-class athletes, toy-makers, sports professionals, authors, human-resource leaders, neuroscientists, designers, entrepreneurs, mountain climbers, and more.

Aristotle once stated, "Happiness is the meaning and the purpose of life, the whole aim and end of human existence." I agree with the first part of that sentence, but don't agree that happiness is the end of human existence. C'EST WHAT? How might you enable happiness to be the beginning and constant flow of energy of human existence? We will address this in the pages that come.

I am writing this book to make practical sense of abstract thinking. The ideas and insights emerge from decades of experiences with creating what's next and learning how to navigate the complexity and perceive the obfuscated happening in our culture. I hope this helps you along that creation journey as well.

My wish for you? That you absorb the ideas in CRAVING THE FUTURE to advance your own personal success and happiness; to help your organizations prosper, your communities thrive, or your families have more vibrant peace and abundance as you create the future in your own image.

WELCOME TO
CRAVING
THE FUTURE
ENJOY THE RIDE.

1 How Craving Emerges

Good morning!

I think of every waking moment as if it were a morning. An opportunity to begin fresh, to have an optimistic outlook and to make the most of your immediate future. When I was growing up on the shores of Lake Michigan in Whitefish Bay, Wisconsin, the sun would rise over the lake, which had the panoramic feel of an ocean, casting impossible shades of blue with a brilliant glow.

Cravings for Experience

Whitefish Bay was an idyllic town. A walk-to-school and hang-out-at-the-soda-shop sort of place. A place to explore, use your imagination, and simply be delighted by anything around you. During the course of exploration, I developed cravings. But these cravings turned out to be for experiences, rather than for material things.

For example, I loved making pickles. My sisters and I would gingerly walk down the stairs to our creepy basement, past the giant oil furnace that was wrapped in asbestos and made haunting, grinding noises. We would circumnavigate the centipedes, the spiders and their webs, and the tool room where our parents kept their liquor, where we would sneak sips as teenagers.

The room we used for pickle making was also creepy, with crackled paint and dark shadows. It at least had a window and plenty of shelves for storing pickles. Since we lived across the street from a produce market, there was an endless supply of ingredients. We would craft multiple experiments in our pickle recipes, and the excitement of transcending the creepiness into creating something we loved became both a secret personal success and a catalyst for bonding. Since then, I have always craved pickles, especially those difficult-to-find half-sours that only a diminishing breed of

Jewish delis know how to make. More truely, I crave the experience of finding and savoring the best pickles, and sharing discoveries with friends. There are a lot of pickles out there in the world, so I can't imagine my craving is unique.

Second, I craved just going to that produce market. The sensory explosion of colors and flavors was magnificent and inspiring, and it changed all the time, so I was constantly delighted. Sendik's squeezed their own orange juice, which was both captivating to watch and delicious to drink. My friends and I were even curious about those spent oranges that donated their now depleted juice, because they made perfect missiles to lob at cars. From behind the bushes, at a stealth range of 50 yards, you could nail a hood if your timing was perfect. Craving perfect timing!

My friends and I would sneak into the debris shack, load up on oranges, and practice the sport of orange tossing. Weird sport, yes! But what emerged was an experience of bonding that was implanted deep in my reptilian brain—both a memory and a metaphor. This experience was all part of how I developed a craving for produce markets and especially oranges, which I use as a catalyst for creativity in my workshops and keynote speeches. Oranges have a built-in treasure trove of sensations; the shape, sound, texture, taste, appearance, and memory are all evocative.

THE SENSORY EXPLOSION OF COLORS AND FLAVORS WAS MAGNIFICENT AND INSPIRING.

I developed a third craving for fish. It dominated our menus and was plentiful, as we lived on the shores of Lake Michigan, which, for all intents and purposes, felt like an ocean and spouted a bounty of tastiness. I would travel with my father to Smith Brothers fish shanty in Port Washington, just north of Milwaukee, picking up whatever was fresh: northern pike, black cod, coho salmon, or walleye. In the spring we would land a bucket full of smelts—breaded and pan-fried—and eat them like popcorn, even the heads and tails. Now, the sight of fresh fish excites me to my bones. I crave the beauty of their bodies, I admire the adventure of people who captured these magnificent delights, I fantasize about ways to cook and eat them.

My cravings emerged from the relationship between objects, such as pickles, oranges, and fish, and the experiences that made these objects meaningful to me. These became metaphors for a greater narrative that would subsequently impact other aspects of my life and what makes me happy.

To this day, I still get a lift from the experience of going to farmers markets and fish markets, or anything to do with cooking and eating fish. I stopped throwing oranges at cars, but I still like oranges more than cars.

More than anything, these experiences led me to explore the idea that many people crave experiences related to objects, more than the objects themselves. What else would possess someone to stand in line for an hour to get an ice cream cone like they do at Salt & Straw in Portland, Oregon? Sure, the ice cream is amazing. But excellent ice cream is plentiful almost everywhere. People are also craving the sensation and social experience and memory of getting the ice cream.

CRAVINGS for Creativity

I have also discovered that people crave stories and the sensations that evoke creativity. At various levels we are all creative souls. In some cases, our creativity is suppressed by societal expectation or elevated definitions of what being creative means. In other cases, creativity is suppressed by our own lack of confidence or belief in ourselves.

From a practical viewpoint, we can't expect people to simply "be creative" all the time without setting the proper context and providing the ideal atmosphere. Creativity needs to be ignited. I have found that multi-sensory stimulations are the match that ignites.

Personally, igniting creativity in others is the "why" in my life.

CREATIVITY NEEDS TO BE IGNITED.

A safe, healthy, happy family is my first priority, but, igniting creativity is my purpose. It's what I truly crave. Discovering ways to help people trigger and use their imagination, to create what's next, to solve personal problems, to overcome obstacles, to navigate organizational dysfunction, and ultimately find happiness.

That is what floats my boat. That is what I crave.

What floats your boat?
What do you crave?

What are the archetypal stories in your life that lead to what you crave in your life? Do you crave things, emotions, sensations, feelings, experiences or the quest for purpose and meaning?

Inflection Points

Reflecting on the inflection points in your life reveals clues to your cravings for meaning and purpose. Can you think about the inflection points in your life?

Ecology

Here's an example of a meaningful inflection point. Our home in Whitefish Bay was on a typical street, which was lined with a lovely canopy of Dutch elm trees, unfortunately becoming infested by predatory beetles. The beetles were killing the trees, so the local government decided to try to kill the beetles. They decided to spray the toxic chemical DDT all through the town.

I was 12 years old and remember the police placing notices on our doors, admonishing us to tape our windows and doors and hide in preparation for fogging. Then one morning, after announcements blared from the police car loudspeakers, we could hear the helicopters and see the dense white mist covering the trees and homes.

I witnessed the toxic pesticide being fogged from helicopters and trucks onto my street. The DDT that was sprayed was ultimately ineffective at killing the beetles, but instead killed thousands of birds, squirrels, and other critters whose dead bodies lined our streets. This story and other similar experiences were chronicled in Rachel Carson's book *Silent Spring*—an appropriate title for the day that birdsong went silent.

Imagine having helicopters fog your street with toxic chemicals and the police asking you to hide in your home. How would you feel? What would you do?

Seeing those helicopters fog our neighborhood with chemicals was a profound moment for me, and I was not alone. Back then, by reading and interviewing people, I could sense that a major shift in our national thinking about the environment was about to happen. Sensing is derived from exploring and connecting seemingly unconnected events. This beginning of the Earth Day movement in 1970 was shared by so many other social and political movements, including the Vietnam War moratorium, post-race riots and even the US government shooting students at Kent State. **There was a broader zeitgeist of people craving change and safety.** The passion was growing for change to emerge. I joined the Environmental Defense Fund and Save the Redwoods League. I also started my own action organization—SMOG: Save Milwaukee or Go—and helped launch the nation's first Earth Day protest and educational initiative.

Culinary

When I was 13 years old I learned to cook, which eventually led me to attend vocational chef school and hotel restaurant school, going on to have several chef roles in various restaurants. After that I worked for larger food producers, creating new products and flavor profiles for restaurants. Through extensive interviews, conversations and research, I was able to sense the emergence of ethnic fusion and nouvelle cuisine by seeing what was happening with street food and celebrity chefs around the world. **Chefs and guests at restaurants were craving variety and ethnic intrigue as the world was becoming more global.** You could see whole new waves of culinary creativity being democratized, which eventually gave us Korean tacos, Wolfgang Puck and California cuisine, and of course plenty of experiments seen in food trucks today.

Fashion

I enjoyed a wonderful phase of my life in the fashion business, driving insights and innovation for brands with back stories such as Levi's and Banana Republic. To be successful, we needed to perceive the future fashion funnel from Milan runways to mass merchandisers, and understand the multi-sensory experience of fashion. There are the sights, the shapes, the texture, the passion, the sexiness, the power of confidence in the personification of you.

When I first joined Levi's in 2001, the company was struggling with major business and brand challenges.

My job was to help understand why customers were fleeing. We conducted extensive research around the world into all aspects of the business: product design, fit, store experience, marketing, employee relations, customer service, distribution. Each insight about what people craved led to a solution.

One of the most important insights was that **Levi's customers craved originality and the sense of exploration.** From a perspective of Jungian archetypes, Levi's brand is The Explorer. The goal related to that archetype is to experience a more authentic and fulfilling life full of freedom—to experience new things and escape from boredom.

Once we understood what our customers craved, we were able to refine our marketing in more authentic and original ways. Levi's brand at its best was in tune with current music, art, theater, social justice and politics. Our customers craved our cultural relevance and leadership. So, our radar had to be keen. Before its fall, Levi's was certainly keen for 130 years. Levi's brand thrived during the independent cool days of James Dean and Marlon Brando, free expression during the Woodstock era, witnessing liberty at the falling of the Berlin Wall, and changing business dress norms during the rise of the dot-com era.

Listening thoughtfully to the cultural zeitgeist in the mid-2000s and deeply understanding what each of our customer segments craved enabled us to shape products, messaging, store experience and customer service in ways that significantly elevated our business with women, craftsmen, teens and other specific tribal segments, each of whom craved something very specifically related to their own life experiences.

Understanding what people crave in their lives and how hearts, minds, and souls connect in this complex narrative are keys to unlocking creativity and innovation.

Recognizing CRAVINGS

What I realized from this exploration is true with any organization. If you are in an organization serving customers, constituents, stakeholders, or family members, then you must learn what they crave. Have you done that? Have you listened to their story and learned what is indelibly etched in their minds and hearts? Have you uncovered insights about the elements that led or can lead to a more soulful existence for people?

You may be thinking that craving is an abstract concept that only applies to creature comforts for immediate satisfaction or addictions such as drugs, alcohol, or tobacco.

My research over the past 30 years and recent interviews with more than 50 thought leaders reveal new dimensions of craving that include human desire for different sensations, emotional states, and a search for meaning. We crave what's on our minds, what's in our hearts, and what's embedded subconsciously in our souls.

Try writing the word here:

How does that feel? I like to write the word "CRAVING" in capital letters because it evokes passion and desire, as well as clarity and power. Those hard-sounding letters seem to jump off the paper with seductive temptation, evoking a plethora of emotional and sensational delights. Can I eat the manifestations of that word from a food truck parked in Santa Fe? Should I roll that word in mango paper and smoke it?

Can we make the word CRAVING stream continuously into our digital feed with shareable stories, collectable images, and catchy songs that satisfy our deepest desires?

The word craving has generally been used to express an intention of urgency in the present moment. We want it, we need it, we must have it, and now. Most often, the word craving is associated with urges that reflect self-destructive and uncontrollable behavior, such as addictions to drugs or food, which can be fine and delightful in moderation, but potentially destructive in excess. Thus, if you visit a bookstore and look for literature about cravings, you will mostly discover ways to master cessation.

However, the word CRAVING, on its own standing, has far less nefarious roots. The word originated in Scandinavia during the fourteenth century, meaning "longing for" and "asking very earnestly." The term also appears in ancient Buddhism, with roots in the word "Tanha," which refers to a thirst, desire, or wish in three different forms:

Kama-tanha

CRAVING for sensual pleasures, ideas, opinions, theories and beliefs.

Bhava-tanha

CRAVING to unite with an experience or eternal re-birth.

Vibhava-tanha

CRAVING to not experience unpleasant things in a future life, which is the portion that leads to the typical association with self-destructive behaviors and addictions, and the need for cessation.

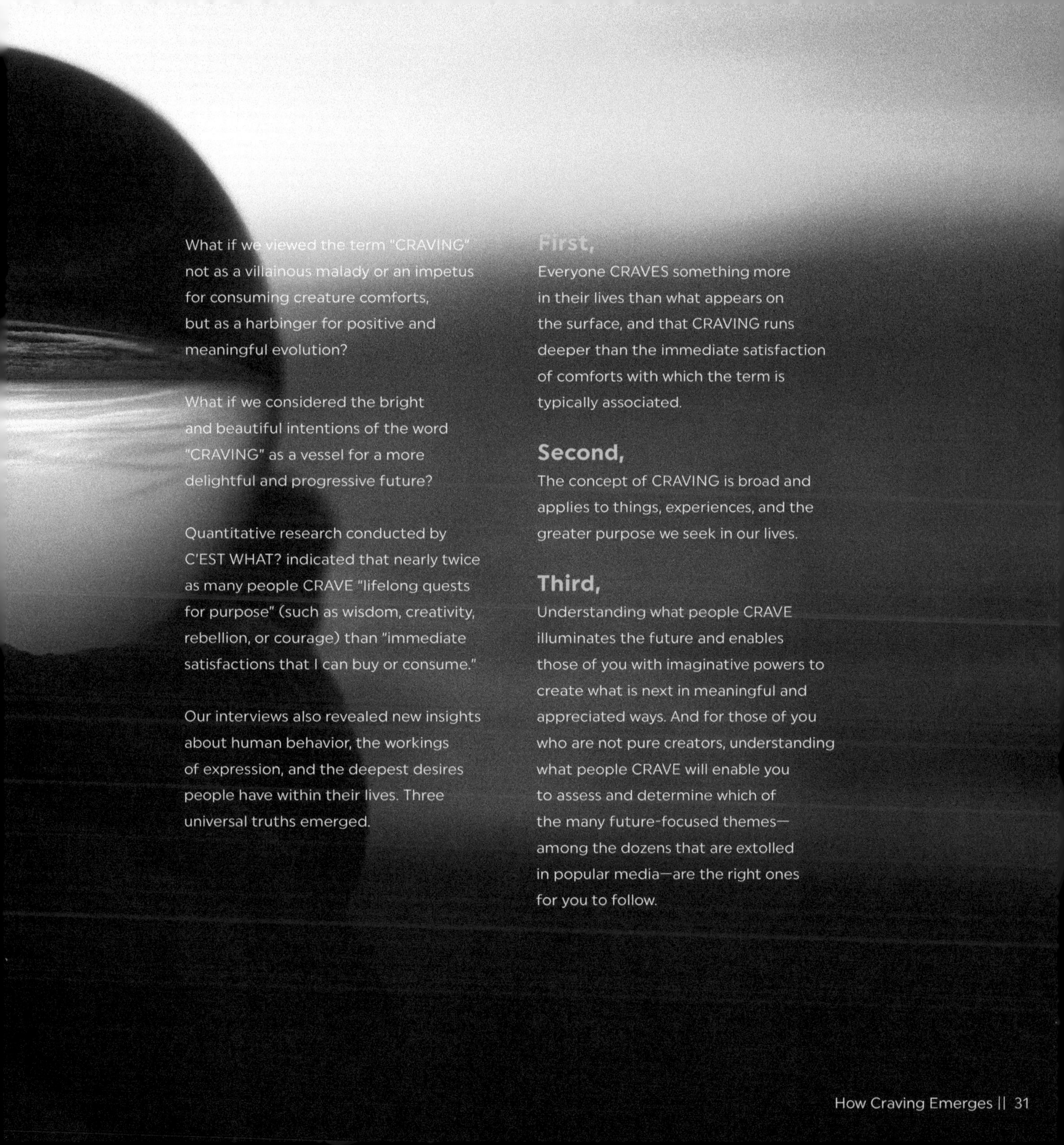

What if we viewed the term "CRAVING" not as a villainous malady or an impetus for consuming creature comforts, but as a harbinger for positive and meaningful evolution?

What if we considered the bright and beautiful intentions of the word "CRAVING" as a vessel for a more delightful and progressive future?

Quantitative research conducted by C'EST WHAT? indicated that nearly twice as many people CRAVE "lifelong quests for purpose" (such as wisdom, creativity, rebellion, or courage) than "immediate satisfactions that I can buy or consume."

Our interviews also revealed new insights about human behavior, the workings of expression, and the deepest desires people have within their lives. Three universal truths emerged.

First,

Everyone CRAVES something more in their lives than what appears on the surface, and that CRAVING runs deeper than the immediate satisfaction of comforts with which the term is typically associated.

Second,

The concept of CRAVING is broad and applies to things, experiences, and the greater purpose we seek in our lives.

Third,

Understanding what people CRAVE illuminates the future and enables those of you with imaginative powers to create what is next in meaningful and appreciated ways. And for those of you who are not pure creators, understanding what people CRAVE will enable you to assess and determine which of the many future-focused themes—among the dozens that are extolled in popular media—are the right ones for you to follow.

QUESTION

Which of the following TIME FRAMES do you most CRAVE?

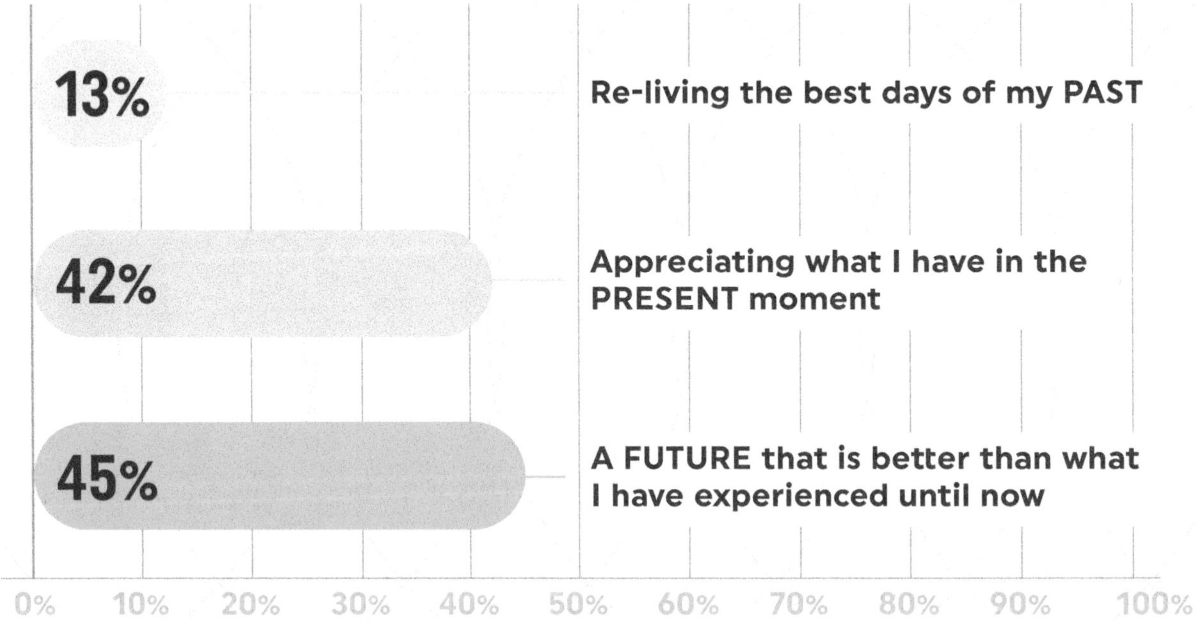

Nationally representative sample of 712 individuals.

QUESTION

Which of the following do you most CRAVE?

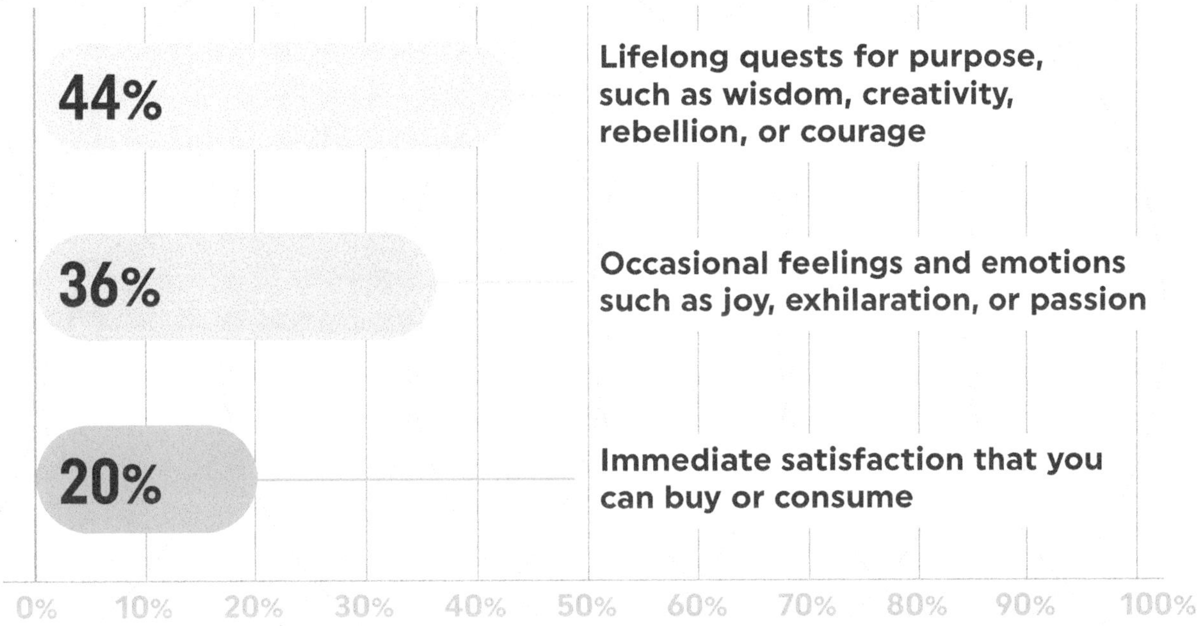

Nationally representative sample of 712 individuals.

Remember we defined innovation as the ability to perceive alternative realities and the courage to move toward those visions.

The process of revealing what people **CRAVE** and flexing your empathy muscle for those **CRAVINGS** will help you uncover latent thinking and tap into your subconscious levels of creativity.

Flexing your curiosity muscle for exploration will help you personally reveal pathways to your own creativity.

Put those two together and you have the pathway to mindfulness and soul, which are powerful tools when creating what's next in relevant ways. What kind of soulful experience are you creating? What CRAVING are you satisfying?

Curiosity is born from comfort with an ambiguous or unpredictable future—and you need that if you're an entrepreneur. Think about the last time you were curious. Did you know with absolute certainty what was going to happen next? Or were you surprised about what you learned? Did you have some trepidation about this lack of predictability? Or were you comfortable with learning along the way?

Sometimes you need to explore the unknown and have some faith in ambiguous futures to get to the really good stuff in life. You need the courage to explore, to push yourself beyond your boundaries. Magic happens when curiosity and courage come together.

If you are reading this book, then you can consider yourself to be a change maker, catalyst, or creative thinker. When we create—when we work for the new—we do so in a collective process. We walk with the energy of those around us and add our own. And in so doing we become **mediums** of what's possible, **champions** of the future, ready to shape what's to come.

Magic happens when curiosity and courage come together.

Tetouan, Morocco

IDEAS I WROTE ON THIS PAGE

GET IT DONE > > >

2 Different Kinds of CRAVINGS

In order to uncover deeper insights about the relationship of craving and a better future, I interviewed more than thirty innovation luminaries. The questions were broad—questions like, "what may be the future of your domain?" and "what cravings can be satisfied in the process?"

Each of these profiles reveals new dimensions and fresh perspectives on different desires for a better future.

How might you live without regrets and act with courageous purpose? Develop habits leading to peace? Transcend creative obstacles by capturing fleeting moments? Reclaim your authenticity and personal story?

While absorbing the profiles of these remarkable leaders, think about your own future or the future of your organization.

What is your personal journey? What are the deep desires you have yet to uncover or activate?

What are the cravings of those around you, and how can you leverage creativity to reveal those cravings?

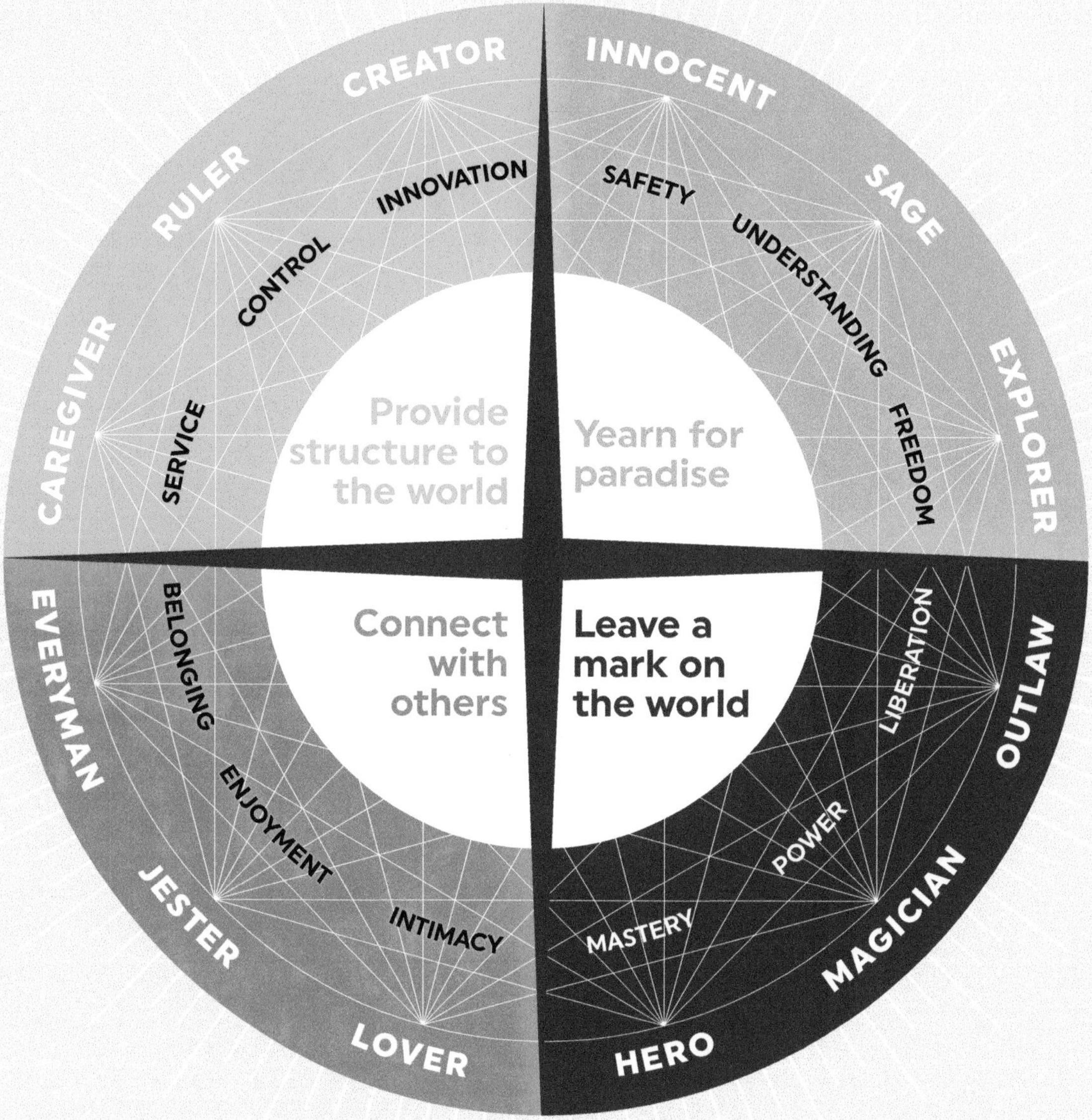
CREATOR
INNOCENT
RULER
SAGE
CAREGIVER
EXPLORER
EVERYMAN
OUTLAW
JESTER
MAGICIAN
LOVER
HERO
INNOVATION
SAFETY
CONTROL
UNDERSTANDING
SERVICE
FREEDOM
BELONGING
LIBERATION
ENJOYMENT
POWER
INTIMACY
MASTERY
Provide structure to the world
Yearn for paradise
Connect with others
Leave a mark on the world

How archetypes shape what we CRAVE

Powerfully emotional and memorable brands, books, and movies often source a construct of creative wisdom known as archetypes that is a wellspring of meaning in life's narratives.

The belief system of archetypes was largely established by Psychologist Carl Jung in the early 1900s. Jung believed that humans form fundamental desires and drivers of behavior in the early years of their lives, based partly on their innate characteristics and partly on their physical environment and early relationships. As children grow, these desires are often suppressed by societal norms, parents, teachers, laws, and political oppression, and they remain locked away in their subconscious. As people enter adulthood, they eventually search to re-discover their selves. **During this search for authenticity, it is important for people to re-connect with the archetypal narratives** that have remained unacknowledged.

Jung wrote about archetypes such as mother, child, and trickster, as well as about natural occurrences, such as floods, and their meanings. Building on Jung's thinking, Joseph Campbell wrote about many, but is most widely

THE EXPLORER

THE CREATOR

THE RULER

THE CAREGIVER

THE INNOCENT

THE EVERYMAN

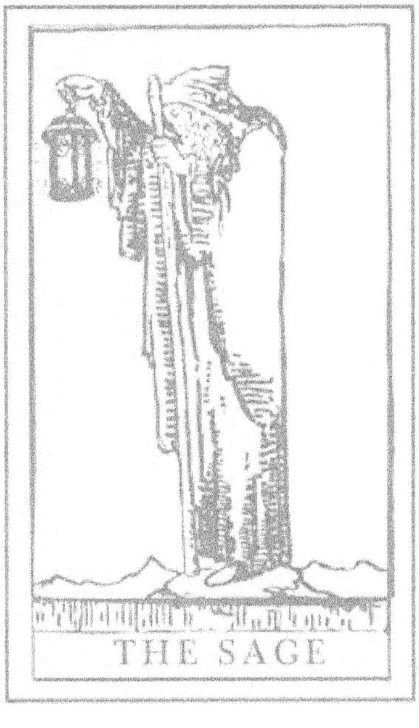

Illustrations courtesy of Margaret Mark

known for his work on the hero's journey, which influenced the plot of *Star Wars*. Many other films leverage the appeal of archetypes. Most of Drew Carey's films are based on **the Jester**. The Lara Croft series is based on **the Explorer**. *Green Book* is based on **the Sage**. *A Star is Born* is based on **the Lover**. Notably, Carol S. Pearson, in her book *Awakening the Heroes Within*, illustrated as many as 12 recurring archetypes, made relevant through metaphors and stories.

Margaret believes that tapping into our deepest human desires through the construct of archetypes builds meaning, while connecting with our contextual needs builds relevance.

Thanks to Margaret Mark, innovative brands have also found success aligning with Jungian Archetypes. In her legendary book co-authored with Dr. Pearson, *The Hero and the Outlaw*, Margaret reveals the ways that brands can tap into the emotional and psychological power of archetypes to become more meaningful. Harley Davidson is **the Outlaw** brand, Ralph Lauren is **the Ruler**, Nike is **the Hero** and Johnson & Johnson is **the Caregiver**.

Margaret and I collaborated when I was leading Consumer Insights for Levi's, and we refined Levi's brand positioning with the Explorer archetype in mind. Levi's has Explorer at its 150-year-old core, leading the pack down a new road, standing up for authenticity, originality, and freedom. Over time, those attributes became values and have helped Levi's brand endure for decades through a spectrum of human intersections and events that cut across cultures.

Margaret believes that tapping into our deepest human desires through the construct of archetypes builds meaning while connecting with our contextual needs builds relevance.

> *"**We have needs in order to survive, in order to feel fulfilled, in order to feel that our lives are worth living.** With archetypes, the power is in acknowledging human need. Fundamental human needs and contextual desires intersect like the double helix all the time."*

> *"**Craving comes in when there are archetypes that kind of go dormant or unacknowledged.** So for example, let's say you are a 28-year-old guy, you get married, you have a couple of kids, and now you have to cave in and buy a minivan and forego your Jeep. You probably crave some semblance of your early Explorer years. So if that minivan gives you the control of music in the front of the car while the kids are watching a video in the back, or there's a moon roof or some other feature that nods to the desire to hold onto what that rugged SUV meant to you, even though you're now a Caregiver, that's going to satisfy some important craving, consciously or otherwise.*

> *"When you have a child, most of us choose to become Caregivers. That's our priority and we're happy with that. And if it means that other archetypes go dormant for a while, so be it. It's good to be mindful of it. If you're not, you can sort of lose touch with that part of yourself and that can then result in some unhealthy or undesirable consequences. If it's conscious and you're mindful of it, you can say, 'Okay I get it. For this period of time, I may not be able to entirely act on my Creator or my Explorer, but it's still part of me and I want to be aware of that and, when the opportunity arises, I'm going to take advantage of it.' It's why a knowledge of archetypes is helpful in personal development.*

Margaret thinks being in alignment with archetypes isn't just a personal thing. She believes it's important for whole cultures, too.

> *"It feels like there are really powerful archetypal currents swimming through the culture right now - most notably, the Warrior seems to be in full force. I'm a big believer—and this would, I guess, be relevant to your innovation quest here—that unacknowledged archetypes aren't unimportant. They're just the opposite. They're terribly important.*

> *"**So when the manifestation of a certain kind of fundamental human desire is dormant, we crave it all the more.** It's a contrarian view of trend analysis that I advocate. Everyone is looking at the obvious—what's evident or emergent in the culture. I think it's more important to examined what's absent from the culture; fundamental human needs that are not manifest. Sooner or later, they need to be addressed. They don't go away."*

Margaret's words are important for the present, and even more important for the future: "**Now, in 2019, the Caregiver, the Lover, the positive side of the Jester are more dormant.** These archetypes are about connectedness and concern for one another. I do think that there are some brands like Airbnb that are speaking to that and are doing so successfully. But only for some segments of the population.

> *"There's an opportunity to create brand entities that speak to affiliation in a way that less upscale segments can identify with, to create products and services and experiences that are relevant by segment, and to provide opportunities to experience unacknowledged archetypes."*

Margaret's bottom line is that awareness of both acknowledged and unacknowledged archetypes—the ones we crave—is beneficial for both your own psyche and the culture in which you live.

Aligning with **Jungian archetypes** allows companies the opportunity to not only be **innovative** but to do it in ways that truly connect with their **customer base,** evoking experiences that are both **emotional** and provide **personal and cultural** wholeness.

CRAVING PURPOSE & ENDURANCE

Katie Spotz

Endurance Athlete, Social Activist

Katie Spotz is a world-class endurance athlete who craves a sense of purpose and contribution. She is unbridled energy nestled in a calm and peaceful core, undaunted by obstacles and inspired by the unknown and desire to try new experiences.

> *"We are all here for a very limited amount of time. That awareness alone leads me to believe that we should be open to trying more things. To try everything once before we die."*

Katie is kind, quiet, and introspective. Yet she's an astonishing dynamo of endurance. By the time I met Katie in the spring of 2011, she had already swum the full 325-mile stretch of the Allegheny River, run across the Mojave Desert, and rowed across the Atlantic Ocean from Senegal to Guyana, a 3000-mile solo journey, alone at sea in a 19-foot rowboat named *Liv*, without assistance or a companion for 70 days.

3000 miles

70 DAYS

Katie did all this to raise money for and draw attention to hundreds of millions of people who don't have access to clean, safe water. What Katie does takes courage—but not the kind that typically comes to mind.

> *"People say I did the row because I have courage. It's kind of like we all have these superpowers, but we don't actually know how to access them. If you don't even believe that it's possible, then it's going to be a lot harder to access it. You're already rejecting the idea. You are pushing away your own greatness.*
>
> *"My definition of courage is setting aside personal fears for something greater. When thinking about courage, I feel like it's something we all have, but life covers it up. It's all about digging deep enough to find what naturally exists within you."*

Many of us face fears in our personal and professional lives. Organizations where we work or cultures in which we live our social lives often exude energy that makes us fearful of sharing ideas, opinions, and genuine feelings. This negative energy can be crippling and prevents you from sharing natural gifts with the world. Katie teaches us to reframe and transcend that typical fear with a craving for action.

"My greatest fear is regret. I can certainly relate to a fear of failure so strong that it prevents you from doing anything at all. For me, a lifetime of regret would have been worse than 72 days of rowing. Fear of missing out on untapped potential. That fear was far greater than fear of sharks or giant waves or all the other scary things I signed up for that would inevitably come my way."

Katie's greatest challenge came on day 54 of the row. She had already braved giant waves, a man o' war sting, perpetual salt crusting in her hair and on her body, heat, a giant tuna smacking the hull of her boat at night, and the physical exhaustion of rowing forever, day and night, as if there were no sense of time. However, desperation eventually caught up with Katie and she hit her low point. Loneliness, despair, a questioning of purpose and meaning. Katie was afraid of letting people down.

> *"I was so worried about feeling that I wanted to quit," she says. "Once I gave myself permission to feel that way and to express that, to open that up, the fear lost its power. So I think the big 'A-ha!' in that lowest low was being honest with myself. As simple as it sounds, it was just the acceptance of what was happening because I tried really hard to not show weakness and I did not want to worry anyone else. So I accepted that it was okay to be overwhelmed."*

“the big **‘A-ha!’** in that lowest low was being **honest** with myself.”

After Katie's row, my team at Levi's sponsored her and a friend to break the two-person cross-country cycling record, which was 7 days, 4 hours and 20 minutes. We hired a film crew to ride with Katie and Sam and capture the scenery.

A week before the ride, Katie wiped out during a morning training ride in the foggy and slippery hills of San Francisco. With a cracked pelvis, she hitchhiked with her bike to the Stanford Medical Center, where doctors determined she would not ride. Once again, Katie was facing the fear of disappointing others and regretting not fulfilling her potential.

Katie called me to discuss her options, which were to cancel the ride or find a replacement—another woman capable of riding 200 miles a day on a moment's notice (there were probably four people in the world who could make that happen). Or, to ride with a recumbent bike, using her arms.

The choice was obvious to both of us. Overcome the obstacle, undaunted. Use creative solutions. Work for something greater. What a perfect lesson for challenges we all face in life. Katie finished the ride on her recumbent bike, with a new support team. Although not in record time, it was an amazing achievement.

Since the ride, Katie has continued matching her physical and spiritual prowess with purpose. She has run several Ironman events and most recently joined the Tour of New Zealand, a mountainous 630 km ride, raising money to fight human trafficking. She teaches us to reframe the concept of fear and be authentic in our own search for purpose.

> *"I have learned how to be with myself: how to accept my emotions, not be afraid of them, and not take them so seriously. I mean, that's what challenges are—you just keep facing these intense emotions and figure out how to manage them. It doesn't serve the world to not be authentically you."*

The future we face is inherently unpredictable since it has not yet happened!

You can choose to be stifled with fear of the unknown, or you can reframe your fears into the opportunity to simultaneously explore and create what is next.

When you are in the process of perceiving new realities—the essence of innovation—there is a lonely ocean to cross. On one side is your past and the assumptions or limitations you've imposed on your thinking. On the other lies the gifts of the unknown that are only appreciated once you cross. In between the two are great expanses of ambiguity, constantly churning with questions and doubts, tempting you to stay where you are. Katie teaches us to make the metaphorical journey—and we don't have to be world class athletes to do so. If you wish for a brighter future personally or professionally, try reframing your fears and doubts.

And by the way, in case you fall into the ocean of ambiguity, it's actually a nice swim.

CRAVING COHERENCE

Ivy Ross

Vice President, Design for Hardware Products at Google

Ivy Ross is a human gyroscope, generating effervescent energy within her social and cultural sphere of influence. Her creative halo is magnetic, and it evokes a broad spectrum of thinking. In her role as Google's Vice President of Hardware Design, Ivy is also a systemic thinker, seeing the relationships between hidden essences of people and the way our seemingly random ideas contribute to excellence. Ivy wishes for her world to flow with synchronicity, and in so doing she brings out the best in people.

"I crave beauty and coherence—being in the same vibration as what's around me—integrating diverse elements, relationships, and values.

> *"I am happier when everything feels like it's connected and integrated. Sometimes, when I am walking in the woods, I feel an incredible sense of coherence. Or walking into an art exhibit and intuiting what that artist is thinking. You kind of dissolve—you could call it the flow state. I try to put myself in situations or adventures where I feel totally coherent."*

Ivy's mind is uniquely ambidextrous. She can flow smoothly between the pragmatic world and the world of creative possibilities. She's able to tap fountains of ideas with the added perspective necessary for bringing these ideas from their inherently fuzzy birth to glorious fruition.

> *"It never mattered to me what my title has been. At the core, I am a builder of products, teams, brands, and even houses. I am a whole systems thinker. When you build a house, you have to think about every part of it. Every part matters. This is the way I think when I'm constructing projects or brands."*

Ivy is also a student of Jungian archetypes. Ivy's journey and her archetypal desires emanate from her individuation as a designer and her career transitions that followed. However, true to form, Ivy is actually a fusion of archetypes—essentially a Builder with a blend of Creator and Explorer. She believes intuition will be an important innovation and human-relations skill for the future, and she's always followed what she believes. She also understands that innovation often comes from perceiving the world through alternatives to codified realities.

> *"Having started in fashion, I was solving consumer problems before people knew they existed. My dad was an industrial designer, and he taught me to see beyond what things appear to be."*

As an innovator, Ivy thrives on creating what's next. She always takes a front seat on the ride (in fact, she's usually driving). She's a continuous learner and a translator—a bridge between the world of reality and the world of possibility.

> *"To me, life is one big incredible board game and we're here as part of the master experiment. Whether we are controlling it or someone else is, I'm not sure. But I ask myself, 'How do I contribute to this world with ideas, products, and beautiful things?' It's not just about what I do—it's also about how I do it with others. What are the things that only I can do to facilitate this?"*

Ivy has finely tuned intuition that comes from her early experiences as a designer. Her original design insights have enabled her to orchestrate the harmonics of teams. She has a remarkable knack for noticing the strengths in the people around her and bringing out their best through an injection of positivity juice. She's an iceberg explorer, leveraging perceptivity skills to see beneath

"TO ME, LIFE IS ONE BIG, INCREDIBLE BOARD GAME AND WE'RE HERE AS PART OF THE MASTER EXPERIMENT."

the surface to each person and team's core talent.

> *"Finding your essence and being really aware of it is a gift you can give yourself. So when I say I look for the gift of genius in people, I mean that I look for their essence. I'm looking for what they love to do—for that fire in their eyes."*

> *"When you watch how people process raw information, you can see clearly how they think. I spend time getting to know my team and using my intuition and observational skills to sense who each person really is. I can clearly see people's essences, and I often notice people are not being used for their unique skills. I wonder: 'how might we amplify someone's truth and use that person for what they do best?' It's the culture and the people that make the thing—so you have to get both of those right.*

"I believe in the art and science of things.

As a leader, if you don't have both sides of the brain in one person, then you have to have both sides on your teams.

I view myself as an orchestra conductor, taking in what my team has to offer, sensing when to call in the other instruments. Knowing when a project needs more science and when it needs more art."

"You can see the diversity of minds and experiences formulating new ideas individually. Then, you can take those individual ideas and create the collective brain of the team. Having a collection of brains is an amazing experience. We are able to connect stream-of-consciousness thoughts and observations."

Everyone in this world generates their own personal field of energy that manifests in our body language, chemistry, mood, emotion, optimism, imagination, and love. Sometimes that energy field takes some time to interpret. With Ivy, the energy field is strong and clear, positive and immediately inspiring. That energetic halo is partly natural gift and partly a consciously honed work of art. How might you hone your own natural gifts into works of art?

"States of being are what really bring me joy.

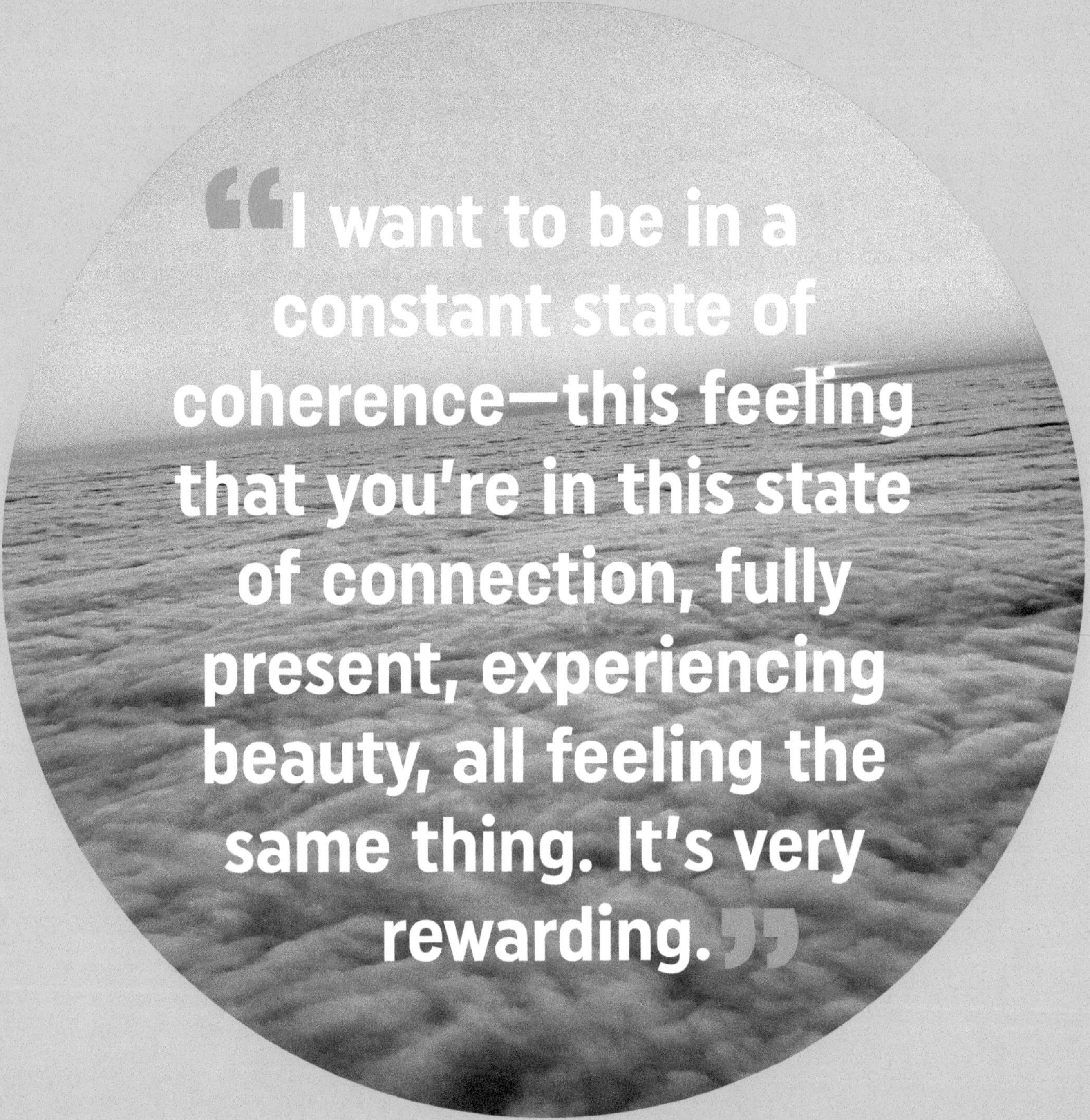

"I want to be in a constant state of coherence—this feeling that you're in this state of connection, fully present, experiencing beauty, all feeling the same thing. It's very rewarding."

CRAVING CREATIVITY

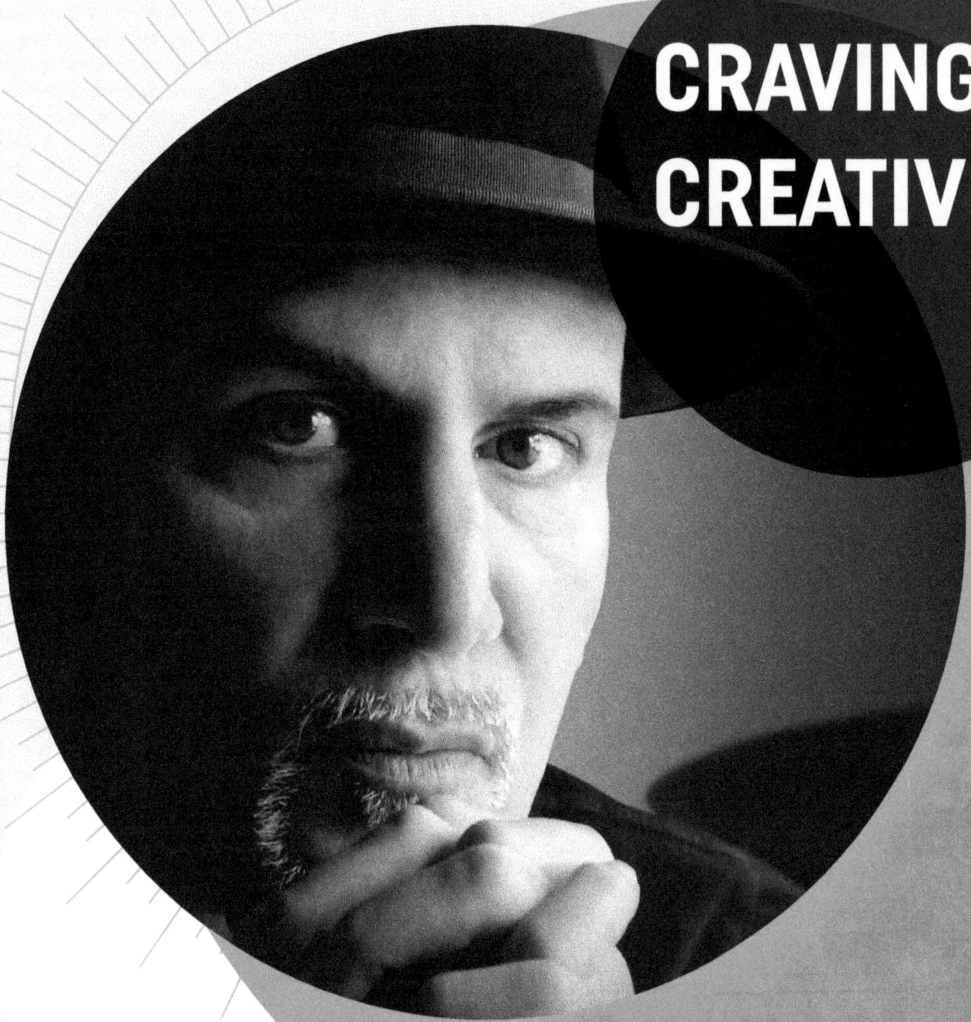

Peter Himmelman

Musician, Writer, Head of Big Muse

Peter Himmelman is a prolific fountain of poignant stories and imaginative music that live at the intersection of powerful emotion and vivid physical sensations. His live concerts engage audiences on a cellular level, revealing his compassion and spiritual core. Peter states it best:

"I really crave to have this deep connection with the people I love and to have new experiences."

Peter is a creative soul who believes creativity originates from spontaneity. He is inspired by the nuances of fleeting experiences happening amidst his sphere, minute-by-minute, expression-by-expression.

Gravytrain

"Like being hungry or thirsty," Peter says, "the need to create arises on its own accord. Sometimes I will just notice something that inspires me. For example, I was at an airport once and saw a young girl, four to five years old, jump up into the arms of a soldier—probably her father. And, he was kind of crying, too. I saw it in all of two-seconds, but it was a powerful moment that led to poetry.

Self Portrait

"My need to express that was so deep, so emotional, that plain old words in a story are not enough. I have this visceral need to communicate a powerful emotion. It comes out through music and lyrics."

Peter is fabulous at fusing seemingly unconnected thoughts, images, and ideas. The metaphors in his music are poignant and gritty. Much of his music is about moving forward, overcoming obstacles, and finding bliss. Peter has the intuitive foresight to interpret the context in which humans relate to each other. He's there for us, as expressed in one of my favorite Himmelman tunes, "Mission of My Soul":

When you need confession,
I'm there to listen.

When you're crossing the ocean,
I've got a boat to row.

When you need attention,
your audience won't be missing.

That's the mission of my soul.

We often wonder from where creativity emerges. Artists make creativity look so easy. Is creativity a considered process or is it an intersection of circumstance and some sort of magic?

Creators and innovators love the moment of origin. It's a rush of validation to know that our minds are in sync with the world, having noticed a pattern of stimuli and transforming that into meaning.

"People who are **actively creative** are **alive in the moment.** They are **fearless** enough to allow their **analytical mind** to recede and the wellspring of information that's **buried in the subconscious** to emerge."

However, it can be challenging to take the next steps, to move ideas from fuzzy and into the phase of fruition. Peter's understanding of this motivation is naturally and mystically fueled, but he is also a realist and understands that many people face doubt and uncertainty about their creative abilities.

Peter's latest mission is to help everyone else unleash their personal creativity and transcend obstacles that commonly stall creative energy. His book, *Let Me Out* reveals ways to unlock your creative mind and bring your ideas to life. In the book, he serves up a fictitious character that sometimes blocks that progress.

> *"Unleashing creativity is really about creating resilience against the negative voice, which in the book I call MARV: 'Majorly Afraid of Revealing Vulnerability.'*

> *"MARV represents the will to live. But, MARV also represents a barking dog, ready to pounce on our creations and place doubt in our minds. If someone criticizes our work, it elicits the same cortisol response that a threatening dog would. MARV is saying, 'You could fail, and the failure will engender shame, and shameful people are shunned.'*

> *"However, MARV is not something you want to banish. Instead, you need to create pockets of time in the day where you can become deeply engaged in the process of following your creative impulses. When doing something creative and challenging, MARV is there, and we say, 'Thank you for the warning, but I am taking a break from you.' Allow some space within a day to write, to have a conversation, to research, to work out, to act."*

Peter believes we are born with courage and creativity. In his song "Hotter Brighter Sun" from his collaboration on *The Boat That Carries Us* album, he paints an image of the place where creativity lives. To me, those lyrics represent the essence of innovation. In creating what's next, you may often find yourself over the edge of what's expected, off to the side of what's been done, and in a place that can feel lonesome. Head toward the light, use your insights and instincts. Play with what you notice.

> *"When good songs of mine emerge, they pretty much just come out and I haven't typically given them much thought. This sense of having allowed these things to just flow out just happens if you allow the space.*

Over the edge of what's expected
Off to the side of what's been done
Beyond what's already been detected
There burns a hotter brighter sun

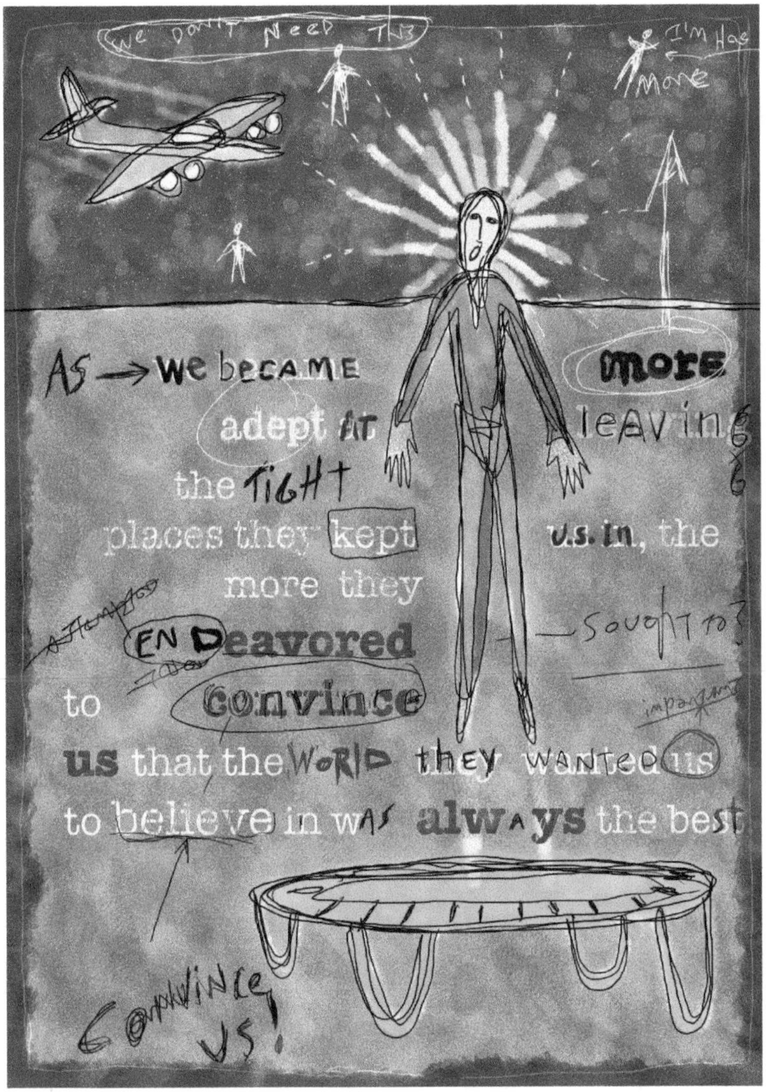
AS → we became more
adept at leaving
the TIGHT
places they kept us in, the
more they
EN Deavored
to convince
us that the WORLD they wanted us
to believe in was always the best
sought to?
Convince
us!

Child's Play

Tangier, Morocco

RIDICULOUS MUSINGS

GET IT DONE > > >

CRAVING TO UNDERSTAND

Dan Pink

Bestselling Author, TED Speaker

A curious man who dives into oceans of knowledge, Daniel Pink discovers mystifying treasures and occasionally comes up for air to share his assemblage of insights about how our minds work, what motivates us, and how we might optimize our lives to be more in sync with the world. His collection of nearly a dozen best-selling books and his hugely popular TED talk ("The Puzzle of Motivation") offer a complementary spectrum of ideas to help us think more effectively. If you crave wisdom and curiosity, Dan is your man.

Of all of Dan's books, one of my favorites is *A Whole New Mind: Why Right Brainers Will Rule the Future*. This book is a valuable treatise for innovators and creative thinkers who appreciate creativity's ambiguous and circuitous journey through the illumination, discovery, and design of solutions. It is an indispensable guide to how curiosity and understanding lead to creativity.

"What I crave is understanding. I find things kind of interesting and a little bit confusing, and I crave understanding; what's going on here? What's happening? Why is this happening?"

Once there is understanding, we dive into the unknown ocean of possibility, along with any other tools we have in our tool belt. While there is certainly skill, stamina, vision, and creative process involved in creating the future, Dan helps us understand the role of timing in our lives with his book *When: The Scientific Secrets of Perfect Timing*. He shares facts and ideas about another human craving—

that of the "right place, right time"—the desire for perfect timing. Is perfect timing random and serendipitous, or is there a methodical and predictable pattern for perfect timing?

> *"I landed on the idea to study timing from the twin springboards of frustration and curiosity. I was making all kinds of timing decisions in my own life. But, I was making them in a pretty sloppy, haphazard way. And that was frustrating. There had to be a better way.*

> *"I was surprised by the absence of any kind of guidance out there on the topic of timing," he says about the difficulty of making the right timing happen. "And, that was kind of the second springboard, which is curiosity. I started looking at the research and realized there was a ginormous amount of research in many, many, many fields—from economics and social psychology, which is where I've written a lot, to things that I knew nothing about. There's a whole field of chronobiology, the biological study of our rhythms.*

> *"And so I spent a couple of years swimming around in this incredible pool of research on time."*

Dan's research on timing reveals examples of intentional ways to improve outcomes by understanding timing in your life—the effects of time of day, beginnings, midpoints, ends. The most clear example is how your body clock works.

> *"What we know about the pattern of the day in our work lives—in any part of our lives—is that we go through the day generally in three stages: a peak, a trough, and a recovery. Most of us [morning people] go through it in that order. People who are night owls go through it in the reverse order; recovery, trough, peak. And what science is telling us is that we should*

do certain kinds of work during each of these periods.

"So during the peak, which for most of us is the morning, we should be doing our heads-down, analytic work. That's when we're able to write reports and analyze data.

"The trough, which is early afternoon to mid-afternoon, is not very good for many things. We should be doing our administrative work then. And then during the recovery—a period later in the day and early evening for most of us—our mood goes back up. But we are less visual and focused than during the peak. And that makes it a great time for things like iterating new ideas or brainstorming."

It's challenging enough to manage our own body clocks. But we also interact with other people in the world. Without really understanding the pattern of other people, it becomes difficult to optimize complementary relationships.

"So during the peak, which for most of us is the morning, we should be doing our heads-down, analytic work. That's when we're able to write reports and analyze data."

> *"One reason for organizational dysfunction is that we're not intentional about timing in relation to other people. For example, I don't think we scrutinize meetings enough. When we think about scheduling meetings, the only criterion we use is availability."*

Good timing is important to those creating what is coming next, to gain momentum for ideas. For some, there is an ethos of "burning midnight oil," born from mythology of sweat equity that implies the harder you work, the more successful you will become. Dan's research challenges aspects of that premise. And there is science to the benefits of taking breaks—mindful, conscious pauses when we allow our brains to step away.

> *"If you leave something in the middle, you're continuing to incubate, you're continuing to run questions in the back of your mind. That also gives you some momentum when you sit back down. Hey, the sentence is already half completed, I can do the other half! And that gives you some momentum to finish your writing."*

Ernest Hemingway was well known for his practice of writing incomplete sentences, walking away for an escape, then coming back to finish the work with a fresh perspective—a method that brought the world some of the finest prose in history.

> *"One of the insights I learned from doing this research is that we are temporal creatures. We have biological clocks essentially in every cell in our body. We move through time.*

"I think the **future of timing** is recognizing that we're **time-based creatures** in a time-based environment. Once we understand that, I think we can actually **make improvements** in our life to **work** a little **smarter** and **live** a little **better.**"

CRAVING PEACE

Margarita Quihuis

Co-Director, Peace Innovation Lab, Stanford

Margarita Quihuis commutes over the North Atlantic in service of finding new venues for peace in the world. As co-director of Stanford's Peace Innovation Lab, she travels from her office in Palo Alto to The Hague, Netherlands—known as "the City of Peace and Justice" and home of the International Criminal Court, the International Tribunal, Mercy Corps, and The Red Cross. Stanford's collaboration with The Hague seeks to inextricably link economics, technology and social behavior to peace.

> *"The Hague has been a perfect place to evolve our thinking about peace. We wanted to understand how we might invent a future that is humane, where people thrive, versus a technology-based future that's been presented as very dystopian. We are navigating this myth that AI, robots, and machine learning are going to leave us all unemployed. It became clear that* ***the concept of peace was going to be dis-intermediated by technology and innovation*** *like many other sectors. And in the Netherlands we found our tribe."*

Margarita and her tribe believe the concept of "peace" needs to be rebranded and reconfigured for the future in order to be a more effectively embraced construct for progress. The future of peace is more pragmatic, more systematic, and more behavioral than philosophical. "Peace as a brand is dated. It's John and Yoko having a love-fest in an Amsterdam hotel. It's peace signs, hippies, Kumbaya, and a lot of great songs. Feels very idealistic, very unrealistic.

Photo by Nathan Fertig via Unsplash

"Instead, we talk about peace as something that's very systematic, that you can design and measure based on behavior. We've learned that behavioral progress toward peace can be measured just like other positive changes in behavior. Anyone who has a Fitbit or looks at Apple Health to track their steps on a daily basis knows this form of persuasion to be compelling. If my daily goal is 10,000 steps and I am short, I will go around the block, right? I'll look at it and I'll go, 'Ooh, I'm at 9,500. Let me get the last 500 so I can get my goal for the day.'

Game designers also know this quite well. Video games are designed to be easy initially so you can have a succession of quick wins. There's no tutorial in video games, they just throw you into the game. People play around with the difficulty and the friction and the emotion. Emotion is key in video games, to engage you."

Additionally, we're very focused on positive peace, not negative peace. Negative peace is the reduction or elimination of violence, the reduction and elimination of war. That's what people think of when they think of peace building: you're going to go into Palestine, you're going to deal with the conflict in the Congo.

Positive peace, on the other hand, is focused on the institutions, attitudes, and context where people can be good to each other.

For example, in music there's an enormous amount of collaboration and innovation with people who are very different from each other. They come together to innovate, and they're very good at listening to each other, literally and metaphorically. If you look at hip hop, you see musicians remix with other genres. So it's new work plus old work to create what's next. That's a form of peaceful innovation.

Margarita has a brilliant method of separating conflict from personality in order to foster more pragmatic solutions. Her concept is to essentially make conflict a third entity external to personalities and codified belief systems, so that the conflict can be solved with the benefit of seeing the problem from different perspectives.

> *"We see a problem that is external to us. And you and I are looking at it like a left eye and a right eye, and we say, 'What's the picture that we see?' We can focus on that thing and say, 'How could we solve this in a really creative way, in a very innovative way?'"*

For example, "**We would never say that a microscope and a telescope could get in a fight with each other.**" The microscope says, 'I can see things at a really atomic level.' And the telescope goes, 'I can see things at a planetary level.' Different resolutions of the same thing. Similarly, people coming from diverse walks of life bring different lenses on reality. And if you can create a culture of innovation where you look at the diverse lenses as a way to de-risk innovation, then it becomes an asset. It's not an argument. If I'm a telescope, as much as I focus, I'm never going to be able to see the atoms. But you could see the atoms. That means you can give me insight on this.

> *"When people are in conflict, they're in fight, flight, or freeze mode. Neuroscience tells us this shuts down the creative and executive functions of the brain. If we can get people in a state where they have access to their creative and executive functions, we're going to come up with much better solutions.*

“If we can get people in a state where they have **access** to their **creative** and **executive** functions, we're going to come up with much **better solutions**.”

Margarita believes that, essentially, micro is the new macro, that societal progress in peace emerges from small changes in behavior that lead to new habits and eventually larger changes in overall harmony.

"I think people crave mutually beneficial, creative, and enjoyable ways to interact with others.

We are social beings who tend to shy away from the potential of conflict. But problems that frustrate us when they're small and easy to solve can fester until there's a blowup. Why wait when you can find peaceful solutions and changes in behavior in early days?

"Let's start a dialogue, saying, 'I want to be good to you. What would be good for you?' And let that person express that. And then we can try to achieve that and have this back-and-forth, saying, 'Am I getting closer to that?' This could be a game changer in how we interact with each other."

World peace is an omni-present, elusive, and important goal. Margarita and her tribe are constantly on the path to help people, organizations, communities, and cultures change behaviors by taking small steps. And there's beauty to her ambition.

*"**We actually don't know what the upper limits of peace are**. When we look at the marvels that we've constructed, we say there's attention, awareness, communication, cooperation, collaboration, innovation, and then there's a collective intelligence. But we don't know what the upper limit is yet. That is yet to be explored."*

LONDON, ENGLAND

CONSPIRACY THEORIES

GET IT DONE > > >

OTHER SENSATIONS AND EXPERIENCES THAT PEOPLE CRAVE

We have conducted extensive research and interviews with a wide spectrum of people to better uncover their cravings. Here are some examples.

"Students crave rich knowledge in an engaging and motivating way."

Priya Lakhani, CEO of Century Tech, Ai-based learning

"People crave a simpler story. People are feeling exhausted by how many different sources of information they need to comprehend."

Dylan Hendricks, Director at Institute for the Future

"People who come into books stores crave an environment where they can escape or learn or grow or explore or step away from reality for a while."

Julie Lyle, former CMO Barnes & Noble

"In a world of being shouted at, we [crave] someone to tell us the truth."

Jae Goodman, CEO Observatory Agency

"Innovation leaders crave time, of their colleague and their CEO to allow nascent ideas to evolve."

Scott Kirsner, CEO, Innovation Leader

"People who are interested in crypto currency and block chain crave authenticity."

Jason White, Entrepreneur

"What we really crave related to craftsmanship is an experience of connection to source. We want to feel in [a sense] of place, and part of a larger world."

Steven Tatar, Designer and Creative Leader

"Designers crave to influence people's lives."

Martin Broen, Vice President of Global Product Design, Pepsico

"People are craving wholeness, they are craving the entire complexity, the entire symphony, they are craving the experience of what full potential is. And, when it comes to creativity, we are craving the truth of who we are."

Dr. Sue Morter, Author of *Energy Codes*

"People crave novelty because cultural product is being replaced by cultural performance as the driving form of our time."

Jess Greenwood, Chief Strategy Officer, R/GA

"People crave the human revolution, the democratization of access to technology."

Darlene Damm: Faculty Vice Chair, Global Grand Challenges, Singularity University

"I crave being centered, distancing myself from the hustle and bustle. I really crave the time I spend being mindful."

John Winsor, Executive in Residence, Laboratory for Innovation Science at Harvard

"College students need a period of discipline, a time of discernment.

They crave a means to figure out how to do what we all desperately want: to submit to a community and an ideal larger than our self, without losing ourselves entirely."

Molly Wharton, Contributing Opinion Writer, *The New York Times.*

Responses to the question: What else do you crave?

"Validation from a place of unconditional love and compassion."

"The one I will never have."

"A future that is based in face-to-face relationships and not so much virtual friendships."

"I crave for our school teachers to get more pay and recognition than these entertainers."

"I crave public civility and a movement of compassion for others."

"Self-driving or flying cars/taxis."

"I crave that people would be more informed but less opinionated about things they hear from a biased source."

"A sense of connectivity and community which I feel is halted due to dependence on technology."

3 Uncovering Deep Desires

Identifying what people want or need through qualitative inquiry is a typical way of revealing innovation opportunities. Ethnographies based on the concepts of design thinking can reveal latent opportunities for innovation and even identify things or experiences that people did not realize they wanted.

For an even deeper level of exploration that peels back layers of choice, try engaging in the CRAVING method of inquiry using the following questions to go with the acronym. Asking these questions of your constituency or of yourself helps reveal true cravings versus simple wishes. Then applying innovation skills intuitively will reveal even more brilliant and meaningful possibilities for bolder innovation.

CURIOSITY

REFLECTION

AMBIGUITY

VORACITY

INNOVATION

NOW

GENEROSITY

Curiosity:
What elements do people wish to explore in new dimensions?

People can be hooked on or enjoy experiencing something in their life, but true cravings happen when the mind doesn't just passively follow something, but is actively curious and seeks it out, often in creative and new ways. Once someone has latched on to a sensation and feels the associated dopamine buzz, they will likely explore other ways to experience it, often in unknown territories.

Surfers provide a good example; the truly devoted want to surf everywhere. They will explore the best new place for waves, like the world-class dangers of Mavericks in Northern California, where monster swells beckon their immediate attention, or surrounded by the massive ice floes and northern lights of the Arctic Ocean. That's where world-class surfer Chris Burkard satisfied his surfing craving: at the 68th parallel in Norway with a film crew producing *Arctic Swell: Surfing the Ends of the Earth*. Reflecting on that experience, Chris stated, "What I love about the Arctic is the challenge that comes in the form of weather, logistics, and navigating your way across a foreign land. I find that amidst the harsh conditions there are glimpses of beauty, and finding them makes it all worthwhile."

Find out what makes your customers so curious they will travel anywhere to explore new dimensions of their passions.

Reflection:

Which memories reflect the best moments in people's lives?

Memories are stored in the brain and often surface later during reflection. Memories that come up often and warmly in people's positive reflections are often harbors of strong meaning. Understanding what is meaningful in these specific moments can provide clues about what may be meaningful on a grander scale. Music concerts are great examples. Lady Gaga at Coachella? Neil Young at Outside Lands? What are those pinnacle moments in life that sparked deep emotion? The first kiss, that time at the beach, the trek across that raging river...Those were meaningful moments because of the connection with people and the emotions conveyed by irreplaceable circumstances.

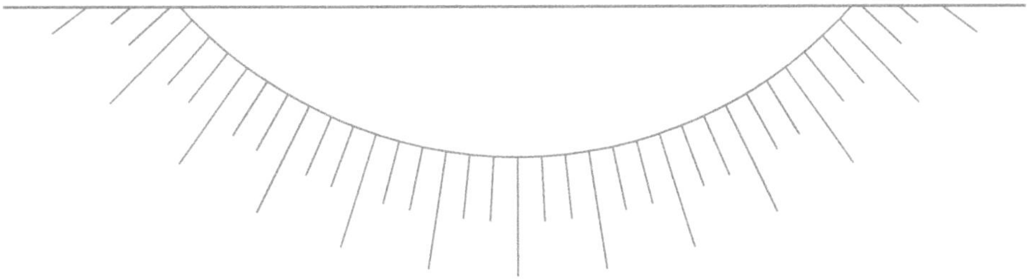

Ambiguity:

What do people seek even when the path and answers are unclear?

People often use their instinct to gain forward momentum. In fact, instinct is usually necessary when the future is unclear, because without instinct we have nowhere to start. For example, the passion and power of running for political office and the resilience required to serve your constituency requires faith in an ambiguous future. Crossing a river of unknown depth, cooking with surprise ingredients in chef competitions, and hiking on an unfamiliar path are all examples of passions that require transcending ambiguous outcomes. As represented in the book and movie *Wild*, 26-year-old Cheryl Strayed thought she had lost everything in her life. With no experience or training, driven only by blind will, she would hike more than a thousand miles of the Pacific Crest Trail from the Mojave Desert, through California and Oregon, to Washington State—and she would do it alone. Wild powerfully captures the terrors and pleasures of one young woman who craved redemption and clarity, forging ahead against all odds on an ambiguous journey that maddened, strengthened, and ultimately healed her.

Voracity:

What experiences or feelings do people seek in unlimited amounts?

Finding the object of someone's voracious hunger is finding their passion—like stumbling upon a fountain whose water can be recycled again and again to create dancing, moving liquid art. What passions can be repeated to virtually unlimited degrees? Video games, bowling, poker, marathon running. Katie Spotz, is an endurance athlete who is passionate about raising attention and money to increase access to water for communities around the world. She swam the full length of the Allegheny River, ran through the Mojave Desert, rowed across the Atlantic Ocean, and biked from one side of the U.S. to the other—all with a voracious appetite for endurance and dedication to a cause.

Intuition:

What instinctual feelings can lead you toward innovation?

Intuition is essentially the phenomena of feeling without processing for reason, like the hunches you get when you haven't even put much thought into the matter at hand. This sensation arrives at the intersection of your heart and mind. "I'll know it when I see it," "love at first site," or "this street looks dangerous" are all measures of intuition. Someone's desire to try blue cheese and sage ice cream does not come from direct experience; it comes from assembled intuition based on related experience—the unconscious aggregation of disparate details into one intuitive pattern. Thus, learning about what people feel is right for them provides clues to what they crave.

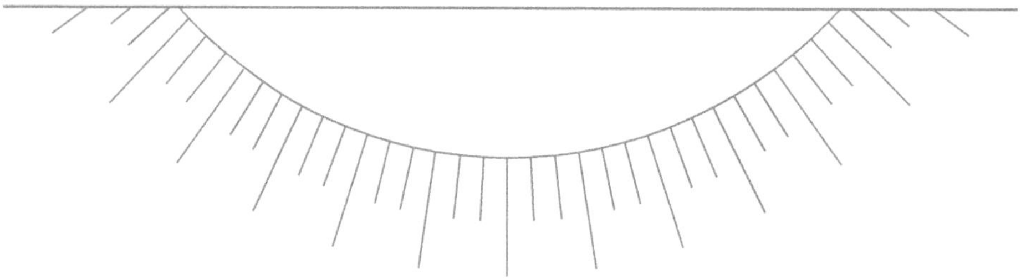

Now:
What might people wish for urgently that would be extremely satisfying?

The sooner they want it, the higher the priority. Craving has stereotypically been connected with a sense of urgency, but that does not mean that the objects of desire are always nefarious. For example, chocolate is an obvious craving, and when the moment comes, the desire is immediate. However, people who are cloistered in a windowless office or in a stressful environment might crave "a breath of fresh air" near plants, sky, and water to balance their personal ecology. Architectural designs are now responding to that craving with biophilic environments in office spaces, mimicking natural settings and even including vertical farms in office towers. When people crave with urgency, they are seeking a sense of balance in order to move through their daily lives. But what they crave could be beautiful and not necessarily addictive or destructive.

Generosity:
What motivates generosity, and the desire to share cravings with others?

People love to share what they love. At a superficial level, that's why people write reviews of restaurants, movies, or vacation spots they love. At a deeper level, sharing an experience with someone close to you is a way of opening up yourself to being vulnerable, establishing a common energy field where you can relate to each other, thereby revealing deeper levels of empathy and trust, which are precursors to generous sharing.

Dr. Paul Zak, Chair of the Department of Neuroeconomics at Claremont Graduate University, has conducted extensive research on the neuroscience of trust in organizations. One key finding is that generating the hormone oxytocin, which Dr. Zak refers to as the "Moral Molecule," is an important element in building empathy that leads to trust. Oxytocin in your body is generated by affection, such as hugging, but also physical or emotional connection and group social activities such as dancing or singing where generous sharing is abundant. His findings indicate that people who are experiencing high doses of oxytocin are more generous with others.

"Turns out that receptors for oxytocin live in areas of the brain associated with social memory. And it tags those social memories with an emotional state." People share what they crave and crave what they generously share.

In summary, asking the right questions with openness and empathy can reveal clues about how to create experiences, products, services and messages that satisfy craving and lead to more prosperous and successful ventures.

ASKING THE RIGHT QUESTIONS WITH **OPENNESS AND EMPATHY** CAN REVEAL CLUES ABOUT HOW TO **CREATE** EXPERIENCES, PRODUCTS, SERVICES AND MESSAGES THAT **SATISFY CRAVING** AND LEAD TO MORE **PROSPEROUS** AND **SUCCESSFUL VENTURES.**

St. Andrews Scotland

BIZARRE IDEAS

GET IT DONE > > >

4

Sensory Experiences

Igniting Innovation by Sparking Sensations

If you're still reading this book, it's likely because you are CRAVING a little creativity in your life: imaginative future vignettes about your personal creative scenarios or the harvest of ideas emerging from full-blown, collaborative experiences that are orchestrated with your team to drive remarkable innovation. If you are seeking innovation, change, and growth in your personal and professional life, then your answer might be both.

While the sources of creativity are often elusive and mysterious, there is evidence that the very concept of creativity and how it is stimulated can be described scientifically.

A 2018 study published by the National Academy of Sciences and led by Post-Doctoral Fellow in Psychology Dr. Roger Beaty suggests that highly creative people are characterized by their ability to simultaneously engage three large-scale neural networks in our brains: the default, salience, and executive systems.

The default mode network, he said, is involved in memory and mental simulation, so the theory is that it plays an important role in processes like mind-wandering, imagination, and spontaneous thinking.

"In terms of creativity, we think that's important for brainstorming," Beaty said. "But you're not always going to stumble onto the most creative idea that way, because you might be drawn to something unoriginal from memory, so that's when these other networks come online."

The salience network, he said, detects important information, both in the environment and internally. When it comes to creativity, researchers believe it may be responsible for sorting through the ideas that emerge from the default mode network. The salience network includes parts of your brain that are responsible for mediating emotions, learning, memory, taste, touch, and planning for the future.

Lastly, Beaty said, the executive control network helps people focus on useful ideas while discarding those that aren't working.

"It's the synchrony between these systems that seems to be important for creativity," Beaty said. "People who think more flexibly and come up with more creative ideas are better able to engage these networks that don't typically work together and bring these systems online.

"What this shows is that the creative brain is wired differently," said Beaty. "People who are more creative can simultaneously engage brain networks that don't typically work together. The default mode network, the salience network and the executive control network — that appear to play key roles in creative thought.

"It's the synchrony between these systems that seems to be important for creativity."

With these findings in mind, I have noticed a significant difference in the effectiveness of different collaborative experience, and now there is scientific evidence to understand why that is true.

When it comes to collaborative experiences, there is a significant distinction between the typical "brainstorming" sessions and the immersive innovation workshops that leverage multi-sensory stimulation to activate the ideal combination of neural networks in our minds which lead to creativity.

Typical brainstorming sessions, which display walls adorned with a flurry of Post-it® notes have generally proven to be ineffective because:

> not everyone is comfortable creating and sharing in a group setting;

> these sessions don't usually produce sufficient mindful inputs that would expand people's spectrum of thinking; and

> typical brainstorming sessions yield nascent ideas that don't move forward, leaving participants with a halo of time wasted.

Multi-sensory innovation workshops, whereby a collection of unfamiliar people have their minds bathed in a combination of intellectual and sensory-stimulating perturbations, induce our collective sub-consciousness, where great ideas are hiding, awaiting a zone of safety to emerge.

The "creative immersion" concept began (though I recognize it only when looking back) with my career in the culinary world. When you go to a restaurant, is your experience 100% focused on the taste of the food? No. What about texture? What about the anticipatory smell? What about the ambience and the delight of gracious hospitality? Culinary arts produce multi-sensory experiences—the music that's playing, the romantically dim lighting, the way the waiter moves softly around you. That whole sensory experience has always been electrifying to me.

From there I phased into innovation in the fashion industry, which has all of the same multi-sensory occurrences, plus sex appeal. Over time I became naturally tuned to the way stimulating the senses leads to creativity. With the goal of perceiving "alternatives to current realities," there are core mindful methods

I have found from my experience which generate brave new concepts to be courageously evolved over time.

To mix metaphors (which is often an effective way to stimulate new thinking), there is a recipe for experiences that enables teams to transcend their creative inhibitions and release a torrent of pent, subconscious imagination that leads to realistic ideas. Each event has a recipe. The secret ingredients in this recipe are in a multi-sensory immersion that triggers future memories, mixed metaphors, new word combinations, music and songs, advanced technologies, empathic emotions, and bizarre images that all lead to the creation of new concepts and, eventually, new realities. Stimulating senses seems to trigger multiple parts of our brains that are responsible for creativity. Well-orchestrated, multi-sensory experiences enable the type of synchronicity that leads to future-focused, fantasy-based thinking and imaginative scenarios projected to evolve five years from now.

Making these experiences happen requires a combination of "mission-clarity," optimal group ecology, and immersion into broad and surprising sensory triggers: sounds, sights, textures, flavors, aromas and physical experiences.

Clarifying the innovation mission and challenge is an iterative, collaborative effort which requires you intersect

Stimulating senses seems to trigger multiple parts of our brains that are responsible for creativity.

marketplace insights and organizational realities. Then you need to stimulate senses and even generate conditions that are equivalent to the phenomena of **synesthesia**; essentially the transposing of senses.

The term "synesthesia" comes from Greek language (those Greeks had such fabulous ideas). It means: "to perceive together" and more commonly represents the ability to cross-pollinate senses. Can you taste the color of winning? Can you feel the enchanting sound of a harp on the skin in front of your heart?

For example, using live music as a tool to generate energy vibrations and enhance the overall mood can generate a dopamine rush, flooding minds with the excitement of creating what is next. Music and lyrics touch our emotions and trigger memories and metaphors.

Giving gifts while live music is playing can enhance the experience even more, generating empathy. Try giving to everyone in the room plush animal toys that can be loved. Soft and mushy, you bet! But, the climate of kindness you generate pays dividends in the energy people devote to helping you create your future.

Food, fragrance, and texture also play a role. Having people be met with unique combinations of foods stimulates their senses and memory. Sliced oranges with vanilla, cardamom, and cinnamon work well. Ask people to share what metaphors or memories are evoked. The elements of surprise and the act of sharing ideas that are triggered immediately places people in a new mental space.

What I love most about the dozens of innovation events that I have produced is the transformative power these events have on individuals. During one event at Banana Republic headquarters, a participating designer said, "You have brought so much more life into me. I never would have generated these ideas sitting at my desk, doing my typical line plan."

This is the type of response I live for, what gets me jazzed. I crave the sensation of imagination because I know that other people crave that same sensation.

If you wish to generate the bold creativity that leads to future-focused innovation, try deliberately orchestrating highly immersive, mindfully crafted innovation workshops that activate the neural networks in our minds leading to creation of remarkable ideas. All knowledge, after all, begins with the senses.

ORCHESTRATE HIGHLY IMMERSIVE, MINDFULLY CRAFTED INNOVATION WORKSHOPS THAT ACTIVATE THE NEURAL NETWORKS IN OUR MINDS.

Trastevere, Rome, Italy

CALCULATED FUTURE SCHEMES

GET IT DONE > > >

5 Memories for the Future

YOU ARE A CATALYST, A CHANGE-MAKER AND CREATIVE THINKER. I INVITE YOU TO SHARE YOUR WISDOM AND PERSPECTIVE TO HELP CREATE WHAT IS COMING NEXT.

When we create, when we work for the new, we do so in a collective progress. We walk with the energy of those around us and we add our own. And, in so doing we become mediums of what is possible, champions of what is possible, ready to shape what is coming next through empathy and innovation.

The following "**memories**" are essential skills, experiences, and proven steps along the journey to creating the future. My wish is that you embrace them, teach them, utilize them with your team-mates.

Creativity is innate, often obfuscated, and sometimes suppressed and then wonderfully released. The world wants you to share what is on your mind and see how it becomes something tangible and innovative for the future.

Some people like to keep their creativity in a bin for safe keeping, assuming there is a time and place for their imagination to bloom. Perhaps. But method often combines with madness to make creativity happen.

In these following pages, I share eight memories—ways for you to easily embed creative skills that yield results into your process. The key here is to prioritize moving ideas from fuzzy to fruition, generating insights and energy with those around you, evolving and shaping to create what is next in meaningful ways.

You and your imagination can shape what's coming. The world is wishing for your brilliance to emerge. We hope these tools get you going on the road ahead.

Creativity Skills

THESE STIMULI INTERRUPT OUR TYPICAL PATTERNS OF PERCEIVING THE WORLD WHILE CREATING NEW NEURAL PATHWAYS AND NEW MEANS OF INTERPRETING THE MOMENT.

Getting in the Groove

When creating the future, every meeting needs to feel distinct from the meetings of the past. We are multi-sensory creatures; we are intrigued by the presence of new sights, sounds, smells, textures, and feelings.

HOW TO MAKE IT HAPPEN:

Sound:

Begin your next innovation session with music. Live musicians are ideal because they add humanity and vibratory subtleties to the room. Have the music play over your "meet and greet." Then, have everyone share stories about their interpretation of the music's meaning.

Taste:

Have your event catered with unique food and drink pairings that create new sensations. How about cashews and garam masala? Oranges and Madagascar vanilla? Or chocolate with jalapeños? While music plays, have people sample tastes and tell stories that come to mind.

Touch

Set up a touch lab of materials, fabrics, and other textures. After a 30-minute sensory session, ask team members to express the ideas and images that came to mind and how that experience made them feel.

How might this state of mind inform future designs of a guest experience?

EVACUATE PREVIOUS WAYS OF THINKING TO MAKE ROOM FOR THE NEW. YOU CAN'T FILL A CUP IF IT'S ALREADY FULL.

Mindful Creation

Mindfulness-based meditation provides a respite that helps clear our mind of preconceived notions.

HOW TO MAKE IT HAPPEN:

Letting Go

Work a few minutes of mindfulness into each meeting. You can bring in a yoga or meditation instructor, or just begin with a minute of quiet reflection — asking people to simply let go of what came before this moment. As thoughts arise, let them float away. These quiet moments encourage the team to honor the present as a path to the future and to appreciate the concept of impermanence.

Become Creators

Guide people towards a state of being at peace with their talents and the talents of fellow thinkers. Assume positive intentions for the ideas coming your way. Help people move into a creator mode, rather than remaining trapped in the roles of victims or passive participants. Create non-judgmental fields of energy. Balance hearts and minds.

IF YOU WANT YOUR IDEAS TO BE HEARD, THEN YOU NEED TO CONVEY THEM IN SUCCINCT "HEADLINES."

Headlines and Connections

Did you know people can only absorb about eight seconds of content before their minds start to wander? Wandering minds are good for ideation. But if you want your idea to be heard, then you need to convey them in succinct "headlines" that summarize your innovation challenge. Ten words or less is a good length to aim for. Expressing ideas in succinct ways can invite others to connect with your mindset.

HOW TO MAKE IT HAPPEN:

Wishes

Try expressing your ideas as wishes. Why? Because it's difficult to criticize someone else's genuine, heartfelt wish, even if it's beyond anything feasible. Deliver these as concise headlines, such as "I wish I could clone myself and become a sheep."

Roll With It

Once you have heard a wish, try building on top of it. You can ask non-judgmental questions for clarity, such as, "That's interesting, how did you arrive at that idea?" Think of yourself as an actor engaged in improvisational theater.

Fusion

Try fusing two or more ideas together to create hybrids. This is an element of co-creation. Harness the collective consciousness in the room.

WE EXERCISE BOTH OUR RIGHT-BRAIN AND LEFT-BRAIN SKILLS TO COALESCE AROUND OUR MENTAL CENTERS OF GRAVITY.

Diverge/Converge:

When it is time to generate ideas and share new perspectives in a group setting, the ideal method is to expand our horizons to produce prolific ideas in a divergent manner, then converge to synthesize for quality and clarity. To diverge means to stray from your mental norms and let ideas flow prolifically—think panoramically. Then, we filter and assemble these ideas, letting them merge into coherent categories that express our mode of thinking in simple terms. By this method, we exercise both our right-brain and left-brain skills to coalesce around our mental centers of gravity.

HOW TO MAKE IT HAPPEN:

Suspend Disbelief

Use your imagination and enjoy the imagination of your teammates. Our goal is quantity more than quality in this phase.

Time to Think

Ideas don't always flow right away. Allow time to generate hundreds of possible ideas—at least three hours. You can use sticky notes, game cards, or any other form of recording to state ideas in ten words or less.

Distill Into Themes

From hundreds of individual ideas that build on each other, we distill five or six meaningful and intriguing themes that address the challenge at hand. Step back and assess the full set of ideas for patterns, and begin placing similar ideas together. Allow one hour for assembly.

WE STRETCH THE CONTINUUM OF IDEAS TO INCLUDE EVERYTHING FROM PRACTICAL SOLUTIONS TO ABSURD AND ILLOGICAL ONES...

Panoramic Ideation

Expanding the panorama of possible ideas that address our innovation challenge helps move the center point further from our current view of reality, thereby generating fresh avenues of thinking. We stretch the continuum of ideas to include everything from practical solutions to absurd and illogical ones, then bring the ideas back so that they can be evolved and developed.

HOW TO MAKE IT HAPPEN:

Restate the Challenge

Devote a moment with the team to restate the innovation challenge. Ask questions to clarify any nuances. Avoid the temptation to provide too much information—creativity flows more easily with fresh eyes.

Practice on an Easy Idea

For practice, let's say your task is to create a new brand of chocolate (the world needs more chocolate, right?). Ask the team to begin sharing rational solutions, e.g., chocolate infused with peppers. Move to analogies: "I wish this chocolate tasted like cake." Then, metaphors: "Fuzzy like a bunny." Move to absurd or illegal options: "Cannabis chocolate steak!"

Thanks, Keep Going

As the facilitator, your role is to keep the ideas flowing, not to evaluate them as they appear. So, say, "Thank you" for contributions at each level, but avoid commenting on the appeal of the ideas. Just keep asking people to stretch their imagination!

LISTENING SO OTHERS FEEL HEARD, VALUING THEIR IDEAS AND INVITING FUTURE CONTRIBUTIONS LEADS TO THE CREATION OF MORE POWERFUL THEMES AND STRATEGIC CONCEPTS.

Empathic Listening:

When you practice listening with empathy, you foster trust in others and make them feel comfortable with sharing ideas and stories with you. Your goal here is to encourage thought partnerships.

HOW TO MAKE IT HAPPEN:

Start Fresh

Take a moment, hit the "re-start" button in your mind, and empty your virtual trash. Turn off distractions and bring your attention to presence, to this moment now.

Engage to Absorb

Tune into the energy field of the people who wish to be heard. Eliminate your pre-conceived assumptions. Listen with all of your senses, for all sensory messages that are being conveyed.

Calibrate

Assess what you have heard without judgement, and ask questions to increase the depth of your understanding. Express an invitation to be further enlightened. Inquire and calibrate to determine if you are hearing what is being conveyed.

CREATING SPACE BETWEEN WHAT YOU **HEAR** AND WHAT YOU **SAY** ENABLES YOU TO SPEAK THROUGH YOUR **VALUES** IN A **MINDFUL,** NON-JUDGMENTAL WAY, KEEPING THE **CREATIVE MOJO WORKING.**

The Space Between

When you are in a mode of creation, it's best to allow big ideas you hear to sink in a bit before a major response. Allowing for this space helps retain the spontaneity of the moment. Be aware of—and look out for—noise in the system that can interfere with your creativity.

HOW TO MAKE IT HAPPEN:

Incoming

Pay attention to stimuli that evoke strong emotions in a group setting, or anytime, during your day. Observe the stressors that are provoked by what you hear. Not every moment is a creative epiphany.

Empty Space

Take a moment to pause upon hearing new content, especially if those messages appear initially stressful. Observe your physical and emotional state. Ask yourself, "What previous experiences does this remind me of?" Then, take a moment to pause and let the stress wash over you like a warm summer breeze.

FORMING THOUGHTFUL QUESTIONS AND OPENING NEW VECTORS OF EXPLORATION CAN STIMULATE NEW THINKING AND EVOKE NEW NON-JUDGMENTAL RESPONSES.

Evolutionary Exploration

Forming thoughtful questions and opening new vectors of exploration can stimulate new thinking and evoke non-judgmental responses. In general, questions about what's working are more productive than questions about problems.

HOW TO MAKE IT HAPPEN:

Different Angles

You can approach the question-asking phase through several lenses, depending on the nature of the innovation challenge. Some questions are more pragmatic; some are more poetic and metaphorical. The best questions are open-ended, evocative, and designed to open up new thought patterns.

Deeper Layers

Leading the conversation with genuine curiosity will help you reveal layers of thinking that are embedded in the subconscious mind. Moving from "what" to "why" can prompt deeper conversation. Inviting people to say more about their ideas in order to open new pathways that lead to more pure and evolved forms of thinking.

Collective Consciousness

As teams create together, you may notice that everyone is "on the same wavelength." That's because you are forming a shared energy field and tapping into your collective consciousness. Catalyze this phenomenon by sending waves of friendship and trust to the people around you, using conscious eye contact and listening skills. Creation can then proceed from a place of wholeness.

Rome, Italy

STUNNING IDEAS

GET IT DONE > > >

Using creativity skills as a launching pad, it is time to move forward into the future. Think about the time span you wish to imagine and create. Is your horizon one year, five years, a century?

More than anything, envisioning the future relies on pattern recognition skills. How can you coalesce seemingly unconnected clues from culture, music, theater, politics, technology, and human behavior? The future is sometimes characterized in science fiction. However, your personal future and the future of your organization may evolve from other influences beyond science or technology.

Creating what's next demands openness, a desire for curiosity, an acceptance of ambiguity, and a willingness to persevere with courage and tenacity in the face of not knowing.

Stay open to considering futures that are not yet possible. Follow the clues that you observe. We hope these tools get you going on the road ahead.

Future Skills

THE CHALLENGE SHOULD BE BOTH AMBITIOUS AND INSPIRATIONAL, SO WHEN YOU'RE DONE, YOU'LL FEEL LIKE YOU'VE STRUCK GOLD!

Defining the Quest:

Developing the right "innovation challenge" will influence the way you'll explore your future. The challenge should be both ambitious and inspirational, so when you're done, you'll feel like you've struck gold! Devote time to refining the challenge as a team so you can move forward together.

HOW TO MAKE IT HAPPEN:

Define the Range

Conceptualize and name your future exploration based on a high level of anticipated behavior so that it is broad enough for new interpretation of the present. For example, if you are exploring future food strategies, try exploring the "future of being delighted" or the "sensory satisfaction."

Consider the Audience

Determine whether you wish to stay relevant to existing audiences or to grow with new ones. This will guide the type of external thought partnerships you'll pursue. Who would be affected? Why is this important to them?

Shop the Idea

Socializing your innovation challenge will make you smarter and more collaborative, yielding better ideas. While you want to stay focused and avoid creating a "camel" (i.e., an animal designed by committee), gaining group energy for the quest is valuable.

YOU MAKE YOUR IMAGINED FUTURE MORE LIKELY BY IMAGINING IT FROM AN AUTHENTIC PLACE.

Future Values

Manifesting your future with a focus on your core values will help your ideas transcend time and uncertainty. You make your imagined future more likely by imagining it from an authentic place. Down the line, this may yield more loyalty and passion for your brand. What kind of world do you wish to create?

HOW TO MAKE IT HAPPEN:

Call Out Your Values

Values define your character as a person or an organization. Which values do you want to manifest as you create the future? Are they different from the values you use to drive your everyday actions?

Influence

How might these values affect the way you work as a forward-thinking team? Is there one particular value that is at the center? Find the intersection between your values and the future you wish to create.

Fulfill

With these values in mind, awaken your senses and drive future innovation with a holistic mindset, bringing fulfillment to those around you.

YOU CAN CONVEY THESE FAINT INTIMATIONS OF THE FUTURE WITH IMAGES, HEADLINES, AND PROSE THAT BALANCES "WHAT IS" WITH "WHAT COULD BE."

Creating Curious Clues

Identifying nascent behaviors that represent possible emerging trends will provoke more questions and conversations. We call these embryonic concepts "Curious Clues" which are facts that exist in the world that have not yet been broadly adopted.

HOW TO MAKE IT HAPPEN:

Scan the Content

Search for sources of information that are engaged in communicating what's coming next. Examples include professional conferences, venture-capital investments, and think-tanks such as the MIT Media Lab.

Create the Graphics

Each "Curious Clue" should have its own page. You should plan to create about a dozen for each project. Create a succinct and intriguing title that conveys your perspective on the potential theme. Find an image that represents the idea either literally or metaphorically.

Convey the Idea

Write about 50-100 words that describe the main idea and specifically indicate when, where, how, and why this particularly interesting forward concept is happening.

Pose the Curious Questions

Establish a few provocative questions for each Curious Clue that will lead to a healthy conversation about its relevance to your project and potential for development.

THE SYNERGY THAT EMERGES FROM SHARING THE ACT OF CREATION CAN YIELD EXPONENTIALLY BETTER RESULTS—WITH LESS EFFORT.

External Insights and Co-Creation

When we invite others to help us create, we precipitate the collaborative atmosphere needed to bring an ideal to fruition. The synergy that emerges from sharing the act of creation can yield exponentially better results—with less effort.

HOW TO MAKE IT HAPPEN:

Share Half-Baked

Begin with the liberating assumption that, whatever amazing concept you've created, it's less than it could become. That takes the pressure off you to come up with perfect ideas and opens the door to contributions by your teammates.

Be Prototypical

You can use your Curious Clues to stimulate conversations with external thought leaders and forward-thinking consumers. Think of this step as prototyping what's coming next.

Cook and Serve

Share these inchoate ideas with thought leaders and forward-thinking consumers. Ask them to add and change elements of the ideas. Your goal here is less understanding what people like or don't like. Push for the next evolution and questions to resolve.

WHEN TEAMS INQUIRE ABOUT THE CIRCUMSTANCES AND CONDITIONS THAT LED TO THE BEST OF TIMES, THEY ENTER THE MODE OF FUTURE-CASTING.

Time Flipping:

Reviewing the history of your organization may reveal insights about episodes when your future forecasting was prescient, as well as times when previous teams missed the boat.

HOW TO MAKE IT HAPPEN:

What's Been Best?

In this phase, team members share stories about the best of times in their professional lives and the life of the brand or organization. When teams inquire about the circumstances and conditions that led to the best of times, they enter the mode of future-casting. Practice with a low-risk subject, such as "the past future of autonomous cars." Ask for your teammates' insights and perceptions of the values that influenced outcomes.

What Is Ideal?

Next, team members envision examples of their best future state in terms of the organization and their professional interactions. Discuss the characteristics of a future state. What's the time frame? How have geopolitical shifts shaped the future?

What Might Be?

Here we share examples of concepts we have been exploring in our minds based on the scenarios that could potentially impact our future.

ASK THE TEAM
TO CONVEY
ALTERNATIVE VIEWS
ABOUT THE
FUTURE BASED ON THEIR
OVERALL MINDSET.

Scenarios

Each person on your team has a different relationship with the future. Some are optimistic, some neutral, and some worried. In this phase, we explore broad scenarios that hypothesize changes to the external environment.

HOW TO MAKE IT HAPPEN:

Convey Views

Ask the team to convey alternative views about the future based on their overall mindset. They can physically stand in a spot in the room to reflect their degree of optimism and uncertainty. Try beginning with an optimistic scenario regarding broad environmental factors that may be relevant to your innovation challenge.

Consider VUCA

Consider factors such as wellness, economy, global warming, social and political shifts, and changes in technology. Then try accounting for VUCA factors (volatile, uncertain, complex, ambiguous). Leave the time frame open for interpretation to see how people view the future.

Implications

For each major view of the future, spark a conversation about why people perceive it as they do. Ask them to identify consequences that are likely to emerge in the marketplace. What are new challenges that could emerge? How will attitudes and behavior shifts of citizens, customers, and constituents change? How might competitors act?

ASSESSING THE CATALYSTS AND DRIVERS OF CHANGE WILL SPUR YOU TO THINK OF WHAT'S COMING NEXT.

Catalytic Influences

What are the external forces of change that are affecting your present moment and are likely to affect your future? Are these changes rooted in behavioral economics, technology, social shifts, ecological paradigms, or...? Assessing the catalysts and drivers of change will spur you to think of what's coming next.

HOW TO MAKE IT HAPPEN:

Identify the Category

Identify the category you wish to address: for example, the future of food. Then identify specific influences that are influencing behavior or effecting changes in business/organizational models. Artificial intelligence might be an example of a technology driver that's impacting the future of food.

Assess the Shift

Describe the impending shift. What might happen as a result of this shift? What are the implications for the industry you're in and the way you've conceptualized your innovation quest?

What's Missing?

Have a healthy team discussion about the factors and catalysts you have yet to consider. What other questions do you want to probe?

CONDUCTING HIGHLY IMMERSIVE CREATIVE SESSIONS THAT EXPLORE THE IMPLICATIONS OF EACH CURIOUS CLUE WILL LEAD YOU TO ALTERNATIVE FUTURES.

Team Work with Curious Clues

Sharing the Curious Clues you prepare based on your assessment of the world around you helps distill some key ideas that may also indicate future patterns. It's also beneficial to have teammates point out Curious Clues in the moment.

HOW TO MAKE IT HAPPEN:

Scan the Content

Pass out copies of your Curious Clues to the team. Have them take some time to explore and digest. Ask "Where is the energy?" and, "Who wants to speak first?"

Probe for Consequences

Conduct immersive creative exploration sessions that explore the implications of each signal for the future. Use the creativity skills you've learned. Some provocative questions include, "What happens if this clue becomes mainstream?" "What if our competitors became superior at implementing this idea?" "What are the non-obvious connections?" Devote time to opening up mental territory, and then begin to distill concepts into themes.

Get Habitual

Once your team has experienced working with Curious Clues, ask them to get in the habit of writing them down—even if they're loose and short—when they spot interesting and relevant developments.

HOW WILL YOUR VALUES MANIFEST IN OUR FUTURE?

Evolutions

Once we've alighted on a POV about emerging scenarios, clues, and potential implications, we're ready to envision our own evolution. Time to create! What will we contribute to the world, based on what we now perceive? How will your values manifest in our future? What disruptive transformations might lie on the horizon?

HOW TO MAKE IT HAPPEN:

Headline a Shift

Based on all the insights, foresights, and perspectives we have considered, start creating headlines about this future state. Think about a broadcasting source and the audience that will hear your story. What is the narrative of your achievements and outcomes? How will life have changed?

Backstory

Write a few quotes or create images that support the headline. What artifacts might we see? What emotions are conveyed? What are some potential new experiences?

From-To

Begin writing some statements that describe where your organization might be heading, from where you are today to where we will be in the future. Describe "today's unique offerings" and "today's ways of working" compared to "future offerings" and "future ways of working."

IDENTIFY THE SHAPE, TONE, AND CHARACTERISTICS OF FUTURE PLATFORMS THAT RESONATE WITH YOUR ASSUMPTIONS AND YOUR ASSEMBLED BODY OF EVIDENCE.

Themes and Platforms:

Innovation platforms are strategic frameworks that respond to emerging changes and unmet desires in consumers and marketplaces. From such frameworks, a spectrum of services, experiences, and products can emerge over several years. They are a distillation of emotional states, ways of working, experience designs, and values.

HOW TO MAKE IT HAPPEN:

Coalesce

It is time to coalesce our ideas into themes that will guide our future. We'll leverage our best current thinking and the insights we gleaned from external thought leaders and forward-thinking customers. Identify the shape, tone, and characteristics of future platforms that resonate with our assumptions and our assembled body of evidence.

Generate

Ideate names for your new platforms. These will be used to rally support for disruptive ideas and experiments. Names can be metaphorical or literal. They might sound like book titles, movie titles, or songs. Try single words or evocative phrases.

Distill

Discuss the meaning of your candidates for platform names. Assess if their concepts have "legs"—room for expansion and interpretation. Will the titles generate energy and help your organization innovate?

IN THIS PHASE, WE WILL EXPLORE IMPLICATIONS AND REVERBERATIONS.

Organizational Impacts:

Future shifts will actuate changes in organizational behavior. Successful socialization and implementation depends on remaining forward-thinking about what needs to shift in order for real transformation to occur. In this phase, we will explore implications and reverberations.

HOW TO MAKE IT HAPPEN:

Action Zones

What are the key functional areas or domains in your organization that might influence or be affected by changes emerging from your platforms? Identify those areas as action zones.

Reverberations

For each zone, keeping in mind each aspect of the platform, begin to hypothesize about how those zones will be impacted in the future or how they will influence outcomes. Ideally, you'll then work directly with the people responsible for each domain and gain a direct perspective. Where are the intersections in this matrix?

Desired States

Describe the ideal future state for each domain. How might they evolve? What new resources or ways of working will facilitate success?

THROUGH SHARING STORIES, TEAMS ARE ABLE TO IDENTIFY COMMON VALUES AND LEARN MORE ABOUT WHAT CONSUMERS AND ORGANIZATIONAL LEADERS CRAVE.

Socializing

With your long-term narrative and platforms in hand, its time to socialize, gain support, and foster engagement in the future.

HOW TO MAKE IT HAPPEN:

Mapping Actions

Begin mapping out specific actions that will lead to your platform taking shape. These actions could include ideation sessions, competitive mapping, consumer insights, or experiments. Think of short, medium, and long-term actions.

Experiments

Your platforms at this stage are still strategic. Experiments will help bring the concepts to life. Form hypotheses about your platform and perform experiments in order to gain traction and learn. Be scrappy here—find inexpensive and fast ways to prototype and innovate.

Stories

Through sharing stories, teams are able to identify common values and learn more about what consumers and organizational leaders crave. Craft stories that emerge from your experiments and foster a culture of continuous learning—a growth mindset. Make your stories specific: include time, place, characters, and a genuine narrative.

Orvieto Tuscan Region, Italy

OPEN THE DOORS AND PEEK INSIDE

GET IT DONE > > >

CONCLUSION: I HOPE

Congratulations on finishing this book! I hope you loved the experience of consuming ideas herein as much as I loved creating them for you. I hope you found nuggets of inspiration that guide your personal, as well as professional, future.

You now have a road map for your innovation journey ahead:

Begin by understanding what people crave in their lives—their deepest desires.

Use your empathy muscles to truly listen.

Determine which Jungian archetype is connected to the source of creativity.

Think about inflection points that have shaped the past as a way to perceive alternative realities for the future.

Interpret curious clues using your imagination.

Conduct multi-sensory immersions to release latent ideas from sub-conscious minds and activate the collective consciousness of your teams.

Apply creative skills to expand ideas in panoramic ways.

Socialize early thinking to gain traction and assess the broader implications.

I hope you come back to **CRAVING THE FUTURE** to refresh your memory and apply what you've learned. I hope you discover your true craving in life and the craving of the people for whom you are creating. I hope to meet you in person one day, have a coffee or some smoked salmon, and share ideas about what is "out there," shaping the bold future ahead.

ABOUT THE AUTHOR

Michael Perman galvanizes teams to think and act differently about the future, leading to prosperity, growth, and positive social change. Over his career, Michael has provided brand strategy, insights, and innovation advice to a broad spectrum of brands, including Levi's, Banana Republic, Athleta, Nike, adidas, Starbucks, the US Navy, Hyatt Corporation, Williams-Sonoma, American Signature Furniture, Del Monte, General Mills, and more.

Michael is CEO of C'EST WHAT? LLC, purveyors of mindfully crafted innovation futures. Michael's firm provides strategic innovation consultation for future-facing organizations.

He is regarded as an "out there" thinker, provoking interesting conversations and inspiring the imagination of the people around him.

Michael is also a sought-after public speaker and leader of unique, multi-sensory innovation workshops that build esprit de corps and generate bold ideas and innovation strategies. He leads teams with confidence to move ideas from "fuzzy to fruition."

Michael craves culinary arts, trail running in the woods, writing (of course), inspiring creativity in others, mindfully crafted futures, and smoked salmon. He lives in Portland, Oregon—an innovation hotbed.

Acknowledgements

Thank you to everyone who has participated in Craving the Future Podcasts and interviews.

Special thanks to my family of advisors:

Katie Spotz
Peter Himmelman
Margarita Quihuis
Dan Pink
Ivy Ross
Mike Frick
John Winsor
Steven Smith
Lisa Schneiderman
David Olsen
Todd Sattersen
Jerry Elliott
HUB Collective
Kent Lewis
Emily Kuhl

C'EST WHAT ?

PURVEYORS OF MINDFULLY CRAFTED INNOVATION FUTURES

Graphic Design, Strategy, and Copyediting:
HUB Collective

Content Editor:
Emily Kuhl

CONTACT

michael@cestwhat.org

Twitter: @mperman

LinkedIn: linkedin.com/in/michaelperman

Instagram: CESTWHATLLC

Facebook: No. Philosophically opposed to them.

For Keynote Speaking: contact Mike Frick, mike@speaking.com.

WWW.CESTWHAT.ORG

C'EST
WHAT?

CPSIA information can be obtained
at www.ICGtesting.com
Printed in the USA
BVHW020107190521
607575BV00001B/2

9 780578 222059